a w ...lay

Topi... ...dren

Aiken Drum. There was a man lived in the moon.

Ouch! I've burnt my mouth!

...man in ...e Moon.

...porridge

roast beef

Nursery Rhymes

Haggis

Can you play upon a ladle?

I see the moon,
And the moon sees me;

God bless the moon
And God bless me.

Do you know these moon rhymes?

Judith Makoff and Linda Duncan

Acknowledgements

The authors and publishers would like to thank the children, parents and friends from Worthing, Shirley and Walton-on-Thames who helped so generously — and Ruth Makoff (age 8) for the cover artwork.
They would also like to thank Joy Davidson for her contributions and support.

First published in 1989 by BELAIR PUBLICATIONS LIMITED
Albert House, Apex Business Centre, Boscombe Road, Dunstable, LU5 4RL, United Kingdom.

© 1990 Judith Makoff and Linda Duncan
Reprinted 1997.
Reprinted 1999.

Series editor: Robyn Gordon   Design: Richard Souper
Photography: Stephen Forrest   Cover photograph: Kelvin Freeman

Printed in Hong Kong through World Print Limited.

ISBN: 0 94788 212-X

Contents

Introduction

The ideas in *A World of Display* are intended to encourage a child's natural curiosity and creativity.

Each topic can and should cover all areas of the curriculum as far as possible. This encourages children to investigate, to be aware of potential problems, to ask relevant questions and to develop opinions, leading to a greater understanding of the world in which they live.

Children need to know that their work is valued. We, as teachers, can ensure that this happens by presenting their work in a well-planned, stimulating display to which *all* the children have contributed. A good display will be referred to constantly and will stimulate further ideas; it may even lead to other areas of investigation. An interesting display table will be well used. Children should be encouraged to take a pride in their display and to keep it tidy for others to enjoy and use. They can be involved in many aspects of planning the display — choosing appropriate backing paper for their pictures, contributing to and arranging the display table, suggesting techniques for the art work and designing an imaginative border.

Displays should, therefore, be seen as an important part of the everyday life of a school, enriching the children's experience and encouraging an imaginative and enthusiastic approach to learning.

Judith Makoff and Linda Duncan
1990

Eyes/Sight

Discussion and Observation/Science Ideas

How do we see? Look at your eyes in a mirror. What can you see? What is the pupil? Does it change size? When? Why? What are the lashes for? Why do we blink/cry? Can you find the tear duct? If possible, borrow a model of the human eye. **Visit** an eye clinic/optician. Discuss safety rules for eye care; aids to good sight — glasses, lenses. Talk about being long/short sighted/colour blind. Invite a blind person to talk about being blind. Look at animals' eyes; do all animals have eyes?

Things to Do

Blindfold a child who tries to find way to door/hall etc.

Art and Craft

'Eye' collage — use magazine cut outs.

Individual paintings from direct observation, matching colours as near as possible — 3D lashes cut from strips of paper, glued and curled to give 3D effect.

'Eyes' made out of gummed and coloured papers.

Line drawings — use coloured pencils, felt-tips, crayons on white paper.

Design elaborate glasses. Look at pictures of Dame Edna or Elton John for inspiration. Make glasses in card, pipe cleaners or rolled paper; decorate with bright paint, metallic papers, glitter, sequins.

Maths

Pairs of eyes.

Graph of eye colour.

Other Language Ideas

Vocabulary — glimpsing, inspecting, viewing, peering, glancing, scrutinising.

Expressions — 'forty winks', 'a nod's as good as a wink', 'blink and you miss it', 'rose coloured spectacles', 'green-eyed monster', 'glad eye', 'evil eye', 'eyesore'.

Create an optician's corner in the classroom.

Inventions that help us see further.

Read and discuss the poem 'I Asked the Boy Who Cannot See' (Once Upon a Rhyme).

Books and Stories

Eyes, Macdonald Starters.

Seeing by Nigel Snell, Hamish Hamilton.

Eyes by Ruth Thompson, 'Look At' Series, Franklin Watts.

The Boy with Square Eyes by Juliet and Charles Snape, Julia Macrae.

The Story of One Eye, Two Eyes, Three Eyes, Trad.

Poems and Rhymes

'I Asked the Boy Who Cannot See', Anon. in *Once upon a Rhyme* edited by Sara and Stephen Corrin, Puffin.

'The Eyes Have It' by Susan Stranks in *Another Second Poetry Book,* OUP.

Songs and Music

'Water Come a Me Eye', Trad. Jamaican, in *The Music Box Song Book,* BBC.

'When Irish Eyes Are Smiling' in *Boomps-a-Daisy,* A & C Black.

Picture to look at

'The Blind Girl', John Everett Millais, 1856.

Display Board

Pale blue background, yellow border.

Letters of 'eyes' — blue on yellow. Large pair of eyes painted, coated with PVA, 3D lashes added.

Display Table

Pale blue/dark blue shiny fabric. Books about eyes; glasses, sun glasses, pince nez, binoculars, kaleidoscope, microscope, magnifying glass, eye bath.

Skin

Discussion and Observation/Science Ideas

What is skin? Does it cover the whole body? Look at own skin through a viewer/magnifying glass. What can you see? (hairs, patterns of lines, moles, spots, birthmarks) Pinch and stretch skin. What happens to it?

Discuss skin structure, the function of skin; skin and age. How does the body repair damage to skin? What happens to your skin in the summer? Why? Skin colour — discuss great variation in shades of skin colour. Why are some skins darker/lighter than others? Skin care and diet; First Aid; skin problems. Look at different kinds of animal skin and animal camouflage. How have humans used animal skins through the ages? Have you got anything made from animal skin? How else are they used today? Is it always necessary?

'Touch' game — blindfold child and touch different areas of the skin gently with a variety of objects — fur, paper, feather, brush.

Art and Craft

Working in pairs, look carefully at partner's skin colour. Try and mix paint to match colour of skin. Paint picture of partner's face.

Find magazine picture of people of different ages; look at difference in skin texture. Draw pictures of an old person and a baby, if possible from direct observation. Use soft pencils, pastels or Conté crayons.

Look at ways different cultures decorate their skin.

Draw own designs on paper, then recreate on partner's skin using face paints and stage make-up.

Maths

Look at people of various ages. Can you guess roughly how old they are? How can you tell?

Other Language Ideas

Vocabulary — melanin, dermis, epidermis, pores, sweat glands, sebaceous glands, sebum, nerve endings, hair follicle, tissue, cells, ultra violet rays.

Expressions — 'thick-skinned', 'skinny', 'I'll skin him', 'under my skin', 'by the skin of her teeth', 'skin and bone', 'skinflint'.

Factual writing about skin.

Books and Stories

On the Way Home by Jill Murphy, Picture Mac.
But Martin by June Counsel, Picture Corgi.
'How the Rhinoceros Got His Skin' by Rudyard Kipling in *Just So Stories*.
Your Skin and Hair by Joan Ireson in 'All About You' Series, Wayland.

Poems and Rhymes

'Insides' by Colin West in *Another Second Poetry Book*, OUP.
'Mirror Friends' by Jamila Gavin in *The Best of Friends*, 'Poems for Me' Series, chosen by Tony Bradman, Blackie.

Songs and Music

'Spotty Song' by Cynthia Raza in *Kokoleoko*, Songs and Activities for Children, Macmillan.

Display Board

Background — green and white chequerboard. Children's paintings of faces around board. Individual pictures backed in black, orange or yellow. Letters of 'our skin' — orange on yellow, backed with black.

Line drawings in oil pastels of old and young faces. Captions on yellow backed with black.

Display Table

Green fabric, terraced with boxes. Items as shown.

Touch

Discussion and Observation/Science Ideas

Why do we touch? Which part of our hands do we use most for touching? Can we feel with other parts of our body? Can touch reassure or alert to danger? What things are pleasant to touch? Why is touch important to a blind person? When is the sense of touch especially important? Do animals have a sense of touch?

Temperature test (blindfold) — arrange drinks in order of temperature — hand-hot to cold.

Other Ideas

Make own 'feely' box.

Games — identify objects by touch (blindfolded) with fingers and other parts of the body.

Art and Craft

Texture collages — use variety of papers and fabrics. Could limit theme e.g. soft/rough/bumpy/smooth pictures.

Pictures of 'things we like touching'.

Modelling with clay and dough.

Make patterns in wet/dry sand.

Maths

Make sets of objects of different textures — rough/ smooth, hard/soft, sharp/prickly, wet/dry.

Other Language Ideas

Vocabulary — tepid, cool, warm, hand-hot, recoil, burning, freezing, numb, Braille alphabet.

Touch an object and describe what it feels like.

Books and Stories

Touch and Feel by Doug Kincaid and Peter Coles, Wheaton.

I Touch by Rachel Isadora, Picture Lion.

King Midas and the Golden Touch, Trad.

Poems and Rhymes

'The Blind Man and the Elephant', by John Godfrey Saxe, *The Oxford Treasury of Children's Poetry,* Guild Publishing.

'The Tickle Rhyme' by Ian Serraillier, *Once Upon a Rhyme,* Young Puffin.

Song

'Put your finger on your head', in *Okki Tokki Unga,* A & C Black.

Display Board

Bright pink and yellow chequerboard, handprinted. Pink border. Letters of 'touch' — bright pink on black. Large elephant cut out, covered in crêpe paper and painted grey; coated with PVA.

Display Table

Covered in yellow and red fabric. 'Feely' box. Variety of different textures, labelled appropriately.

Hair

hair in ringlets

curly hair

spiky hair

Discussion and Observation/Science Ideas

Look at your hair or your friend's hair — what does it feel like? Is it long/short/curly/straight/wavy? Why is some hair curly and some straight? What colour is your hair? Compare hair of newborn baby and older person's hair. Why do we have hair? Do we have hair on other parts of our bodies? Hair care — the importance of regular washing and brushing and keeping brushes and combs clean. What are head lice? Have you ever had nits? How can we prevent the spread of head lice? Invite health visitor to talk about hair care. Look at different customs and traditions of hair styles throughout the world. Discuss hairstyles in history, and hair and work: which jobs require hair to be covered and tied back for reasons of health/safety? Hair and fashion. Look at animals' hair/fur.

Science Activities

Compare wet and dry hair — appearance/length/texture. How strong is hair? Use a single long hair to suspend various objects.

Art and Craft

Hair styles — paint pictures of faces. Use different techniques for making hair:—

Curly hair — printing with small lids/pencil ends for tight curls. Wood shavings, pasta curls, curled paper.

Wavy hair — paint or comb 'waves'.

Straight hair — wool, printing with edge of card, collage of spaghetti, drawing with crayons or oil pastels.

Decorate 'hair' as appropriate — use bows, foil slides, glitterstars, glitter, sequins, ribbons, beads, traditional headdresses.

Hair in stories — illustrate scenes from — Rapunzel, The Twits, The Hairy Toe, Snow White and Rose Red, Mollie Whuppie.

Design your own hairstyle.

Maths

Compare favourite shampoos. Which is most/least popular? Why? Record results.

Graph of hair colour/type.

Hair

Other Ideas

Invite a parent to style a child's hair by braiding, curling or covering hair with turban.

Other Language Ideas

Vocabulary — follicle, shaft, pigment, blow-dry, perm, crew-cut, short back and sides, bob, French pleat, curling tongs, crimpers, cut, snip.

Expressions — 'split hairs', 'to tear one's hair out', 'not to turn a hair', 'hairy', 'hair raising'.

Make a concertina book showing how hair fashion has changed through the ages.

Books and Stories

Look at Hair by Ruth Thomson, Franklin Watts.
Straight Hair, Curly Hair by Augusta Goldin, A & C Black.
The Hair Book by Graham Tether and Ron McKie, Collins Beginner Books.
Great Tales from Long Ago — Rip Van Winkle retold by Catherine Storr, Methuen Children's Books.
Samson retold by Catherine Storr, Franklin Watts.
The Twits by Roald Dahl, Puffin.
Mollie Whuppie by Walter de la Mare, Picture Puffin.
The Hairy Toe by Amelia Rosato, Picture Corgi.

Poems and Rhymes

'Hair' by Max Fatchen in *Rhyme Time 2,* Beaver Books.
'Haircut' by Allan Ahlberg in *Please Mrs. Butler,* Puffin.
'The School Nurse' by Allan Ahlberg in *Please Mrs. Butler,* Puffin.

Songs and Music

'Hair' in *Music Box Song Book,* BBC Books.
'Johnny, get your hair combed', *Music Box Song Book,* as above.

Picture to look at

'Combing the Hair', Degas.

Display Board

Background — red and white chequerboard. Border — printed in fluorescent colours. Letters of 'hair' — yellow on black.

Display Table

Red and yellow fabric. Hair care items, hair decoration, toy head with hair, rollers, 'nit' poster.

Being ill

Discussion and Observation/Science Ideas

Who has been ill? What was the matter? How did you feel? Discuss illnesses — those needing doctor's attention and those that can be treated without. Infectious diseases caused by germs — stress the importance of good hygiene practices. Hospital — who has been an in-patient? Ask local health visitor or nurse to talk to children about going into hospital. Discuss the body's defence mechanisms against disease. Vaccinations; medicines — benefits and dangers — stress safety aspect. Function of pain. Why do children in the Third World die from diseases like measles whilst we do not? Compare standards of health.care.

Art and Craft

Draw or paint pictures of themselves ill in bed, at home or in hospital.
'Fantasy' germs — create own collage or 3D germs using paint, glitter, bubble packing, dough, polystyrene shapes, other junk materials.
Make hygiene posters and invent captions for them.
Models of stretchers, ambulances with doors that open, wheelchairs with moving wheels. Use boxes, cotton reels, card, dowelling, fabric, etc.

Maths

Take temperatures on foreheads using digital display thermometer in early morning and afternoon. Is there any difference in body temperature?

Other Language Ideas

Vocabulary — infection, disease, bacteria, antibody, epidemic, symptom, diagnose, operation, anaesthetic, thermometer, stethoscope; names of illnesses.
What it feels like to be ill.
What makes you feel ill? — loud noises, petrol smells, travelling, eating too much, heat or cold.
Set up hospital in corner of room, using dolls etc.

People who work in a hospital, including the vital work of the ambulance crew.
Being ill long ago.

Drama

Group work — improvise story where child is in pain, tells parents, is taken to hospital by ambulance. What happens next? Use children's own language and ideas.

Books and Stories

Going into Hospital by Althea, Dinosaur Publications.
The Ambulancewoman by Anne Stewart, 'Cherrystones' Series, Hamish Hamilton.
Who's Ill Today? by Lynne Cherry, Beaver Books, Arrow Books.
I Don't Feel Very Well by Franz Brandenberg, Picture Puffin.
Florence Nightingale by Richard Tames, Franklin Watts.

Poems and Rhymes

'The Vulture' by Hilaire Belloc, *A First Poetry Book,* OUP.
'When Dad Felt Bad' by Charles Causeley, *A First Poetry Book,* OUP.

Songs and Music

'I Think I've Caught a Cold', *Harlequin,* A & C Black.
'Doctor, Doctor' by David Moses in *Mrs. Macaroni,* Macmillan Education.

Picture to look at

'The Sick Child', Edvard Munch, 1907.

Display Board

Large picture of hospital scene. Background — any bright colour. Letters of 'Being ill in our school hospital' — white on black or contrast colour. Beds, people — fabric, collage, paint.

Display Table

Children's dolls dressed as doctors, nurses and patients. Real and toy medical equipment. Book of children's writing; books and stories.

Staying Healthy

Discussion and Observation/Science Ideas

What does being healthy/unhealthy mean? How can you tell if you are healthy? What signs indicate good or bad health? Discuss smoking and health. Ways of keeping healthy — discuss the importance of diet, sleep, exercise, regular dentist/optician visit; clinic visit for babies and toddlers, school clinics. Vaccinations, preventative medicine and public health. Role of G.P., school nurse, health visitor, community midwife, dentist, optician, dietician. Stress the need for hygiene — personal, and in food preparation/handling, of vital importance in controlling spread of infection — correct, safe storage and preparation procedures for different foods. Discuss how harmful bacteria can be killed. Stress need to keep animals' feeding utensils and food separate from ours, and the dangers of pets' excreta — how can it be disposed of safely and responsibly?

Art and Craft

Design poster/picture depicting one of the areas of discussion.

Design packaging for a mild washing powder/washing up liquid/soap which has no unnecessary additives — colours, brighteners, bleaches, perfumes.

Collages — portraying different food groups. Use magazine cut-outs, own crayon and felt-tip drawings, fabrics, foam, fruit prints, variety of papers of different textures and colours.

Painting of doctors, nurses, dentists, health visitors.

Maths

Time —.how many hours sleep do you have each night? Weigh any children/members of staff who are happy to be weighed. Are any of us overweight?

Other Language Ideas

Set up 'clinic' in corner of classroom. Include equipment for eyetests, large scales for weighing, mirror, 'diet sheets', leaflets and posters obtained from local clinic,

play syringes for vaccinations.

Visit supermarket to look at range of foods. Which are fresh? What does 'organic' mean?

Other Activities

Group work — each group to plan, shop for and prepare a simple balanced meal. Invite others in class to sample and discuss the results!

Handwashing session — learn how to wash hands properly, rinse and dry them.

Books and Stories

Health and Food by Dorothy Baldwin, Wayland.
Germs Make Me Sick by Melvin Berger, A & C Black.
The School Nurse, 'My School' Series, Wayland.

Poems and Rhymes

'The Story of Augustus who would not have any Soup', in 'Betsy Pud' by Jean Kenward, *A Very First Poetry Book,* OUP.
'Beware' by John Kitching in *Another Second Poetry Book,* OUP.

Songs and Music

'Food' by Brenda Piper in *Sing as You Grow,* Ward Lock Educational.

Display Board

Background — bright orange or yellow paper. Letters of 'staying healthy' in red or white on black. Children's individual pictures mounted in black and contrasting colour. Child-size figures in fabric collage — paint faces and limbs and coat with PVA.

Display Table

Middle Section — fabric to match board. **Left-hand side** (healthy food) — green fabric. **Right-hand side** (junk food) — red fabric. **Food** — make out of dough or papier mâché, hardened, painted and varnished; paper, fabric, foam. Empty food containers. Items connected with exercise and washing. Book of children's writing.

Teeth

Discussion and Observation/Science Ideas

Look at your teeth in a mirror. Can you see different shaped teeth? Why are teeth these shapes? Think of the different ways we use our teeth for eating — biting, chewing. Look at position of teeth in jaws of human skull. How many times a day do you clean your teeth? When is the best time to clean them? Invite dentist in to talk about tooth care. Which foods are good/bad for teeth? Why do some people have false teeth? Practise cleaning teeth thoroughly and correctly. Find out about dental hygiene and dentistry in the past. Look at pictures of animals' teeth. How can you tell if they are carnivores, omnivores or herbivores? Do animals get toothache?

Art and Craft

Paint, draw, crayon a face with open mouth. Make teeth out of squares of white paper or card.

Design a poster to promote good dental hygiene.

Make plasticine faces — pink/brown for flesh, white for teeth.

Collage of foods that are good/bad for teeth — use magazine cut-outs; make **sweets** — Plasticine wrapped in foil and Cellophane or old sweet wrappers; **cakes** — thin foam cut into appropriate shapes and decorated; **lollipops** — gummed or marbled paper and sticks; **fizzy drinks** — make orange or yellow bubble prints, add glitter and cut into bottle or beaker shapes.

Maths

Graphs — favourite toothpaste/toothbrush colour.

Count your teeth. How many have you lost?

Other Language Ideas

Vocabulary — incisors, canines, premolars, molars, plaque, tartar, dentine, crown, root pulp, gum, enamel. Look at tooth structure. Draw a diagram and label parts. Write a slogan for your poster.

Books and Stories

Jessica Goes to the Dentist by Mike Stern, A & C Black.
Look at Teeth by Henry Pluckrose, Franklin Watts.
Teeth, Macdonald Starters.
The Tooth Ball by Philippa Pearce, Picture Puffin.
The Tale of the Tooth Fairy by Helen East, Macdonald Children's Books.

Poems and Rhymes

'Oh, I Wish I'd Looked After me Teeth' by Pam Ayres in *I Like This Poem,* Puffin.
'The Dentist' by Judith Nicholls, in *Another First Poetry Book,* OUP.

Songs and Music

'Wobbly Tooth' by Jane Sebba in *Playalong Songs,* Hamish Hamilton.

Display Board

White background, red crêpe border. Letters of 'teeth' — white on red. Large 3D mouth made of crumpled newspaper, painted red and coated with PVA. 'Teeth' cut out of white card or thin polystyrene. Giant tube of toothpaste — old white sheet cut and sewn into tube shape — stuffed with newspaper. Flower pot for cap. Giant toothbrush made out of card.

Display Table

Red or white fabric. Large mirror with label 'Look at your teeth'; toothbrushes, toothpaste, dental floss, dental mirror, bowl of fruit and vegetables.

Hands

Discussion and Observation/Science Ideas

Look at your hands — how many fingers, thumbs? Structure of hands — joints, palms, knuckles, index fingers. Look at and compare fingerprints. What are our hands used for? Keeping hands warm. Keeping hands and nails clean. How can we help people with our hands? Look at people as they talk — what do they do with their hands? Hand jewellery — look at ways different cultures decorate their hands.

Art and Craft

Handprints — use brightly coloured thick paint, or black paint on white/white paint on black.

Use handprint technique to make pictures, e.g. hedgehogs, flowers, hair etc.

Paper collage — cut around hands and build up a collage picture.

Line drawings from observation — study hands in different positions.

Paint and decorate paper gloves/mittens. Use bright paint and a variety of collage materials.

Maths

Pairs of hands.

Counting in 5's and 10's.

Area — draw around hand on squared paper.

Measuring with hand-spans.

Other Language Ideas

Rhyming words: hand, sand etc.

Use of hands in sign language.

Expressions — 'handy', 'singlehanded', 'knuckle under', 'hand in hand', 'lend a hand', 'hand in glove', 'you've put your finger on it'.

Books and Stories

Look at Hands by Ruth Thomson, Franklin Watts.

Don't Touch by Suzy Kline, Picture Puffin.

Poems and Rhymes

'This is the Hand' by Michael Rosen in *A First Poetry Book,* OUP.

'Hands' by Peter Young in *A First Poetry Book,* OUP.

Songs and Music

'Kaigal-Hands' in *Tinderbox,* A & C Black.

'Clap Hands' in *The Clarendon Book of Singing Games, Book 1,* OUP.

Display Board

White background, pink crêpe paper border. Letters of 'hands' — pink on black.

Display Table

Pink and lilac fabric. Hand care products, gloves, mittens, muff, jewellery.

Blood

Discussion and Observation/Science Ideas

What happens when you fall over and cut your knee? Who has had a nose bleed? What makes the bleeding stop? What do red blood cells look like? What do white cells do? How many red/white cells are in your body? What is plasma? What does blood do? What pumps the blood round the body? Do you know your blood group? Talk about First Aid. Visit from St. John's Ambulance Service member.

Art and Craft

Paint red/white blood cells. Coat with PVA.

Collages of red blood cells — shiny fabric, Cellophane, foil — glued on to yellow paper. Could sprinkle with red glitter.

Paint or crayon a picture of a cut knee, elbow, head etc. Use paint to achieve different effects e.g. thick red paint, thin drippy paint. Coat with PVA.

Pictures showing how fibrin forms a 'net' — on round white paper make collages of red and white cells (use fabric and paper); overprint in yellow with card edge to give 'net' effect.

'Blood' pictures — on wet paper, drop thin red paint or ink.

Maths

Capacity — estimate how much blood in *own* body. Estimate lengths of bandages needed to bandage finger, arm or knee of friend. (Work in twos.)

Other Language Ideas

Vocabulary — clot, congeal, haemoglobin, spleen, bone marrow, lymph, vein, artery, rhesus, haemophiliac, platelets, fibrin.
Factual writing.

Books and Stories

The Heart and Blood by Brian R. Ward, Franklin Watts.
On the Way Home by Jill Murphy, Picture Mac.
Just Awful by Alma Marshak Whitney, Picture Lion.

Poems and Rhymes

'Vampire Visit' by Doug Macleod in *Another Second Poetry Book,* OUP.
'When Dracula Went to the Blood Bank' by Jack Prelutsky, *Another Second Poetry Book,* OUP.

Songs and Music

'Grazed Knee' in *The Music Fun Shop,* Hamish Hamilton.

Display Board

Background — red and white chequerboard, yellow crêpe border printed with red circles. Letters of 'blood' — red foil on yellow. Large figure showing flow of blood.

Display Table

Covered in red shiny fabric/red net. First Aid kit. Dolls and teddies bandaged.

Ears/Hearing

Discussion and Observation/Science Ideas

Sit still and listen! What can you hear? Can you hear a pin drop? How do we hear? Look at drawing/model of an ear. How does the ear work? Why is it the shape it is? How do sound waves reach the ears? What is noise? Why are loud noises potentially harmful? Importance of keeping noise levels down and of *listening* to people. What do you enjoy/dislike listening to? Classify sounds — transport sounds, nature sounds, warning and danger sounds. Who has had a hearing test? How was it done? Invite an audiologist to talk to children. What is it like to be deaf? What problems occur? Invite someone to demonstrate sign language.

Art and Craft

Individual pictures of faces — accentuate ears with felt, foam, gummed paper.
Pictures of animals/objects that make sounds.
Design earrings.
Make sound mobiles/wind chimes — use bottle tops, budgie bells, large buttons, metal scrap. Which sounds do you like best?

Maths

Graphs showing sounds we like/dislike.
Sets of things that make loud/soft noises.

Other language Ideas

Vocabulary — loud, soft, silent, noisy, shrill, piercing, echo, resonate, vibrate, sound waves.
Go on a 'listening' walk. Write which sounds you heard.
Alliterative phrases and sentences.

Books and Stories

Hearing by Henry Pluckrose, in 'Thinkabout' Series, Franklin Watts.
The Boy Who Couldn't Hear by Freddy Bloom, Bodley Head.

Poems and Rhymes

'The Sounds in the Evening' by Eleanor Farjeon in *A First Poetry Book,* OUP.
'Noises in the Night' by Lilian McCrea in *The Book of a Thousand Poems,* Bell & Hyman.

Songs and Music

'Sound Song' in *Tinderbox*, A & C Black.
'I like Peace, I like Quiet' in *Songs from Playschool,* A & C Black.

Musical Activities

Listen to short excerpts from different pieces of music. Which did you enjoy most? Why?
Listening games — play 'Chinese whispers' and 'Squeak piggy, squeak'.

Display Board

Background — pale pink or white, red crêpe border.
Letters of 'ears' — pink on red.

Display Table

Covered in red and white fabric. Sound tracks game and tape recorder. Bottles with different water levels, for making sounds, plus beater.

Tongue/Taste

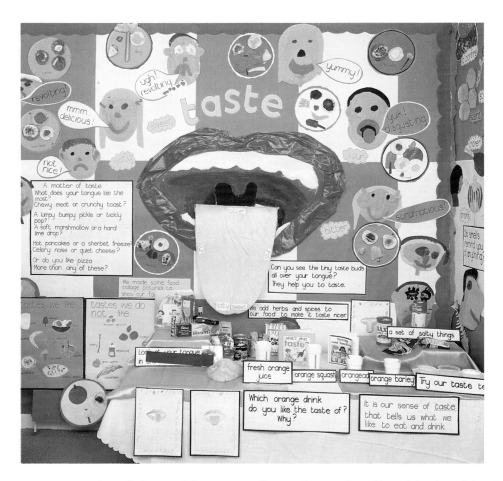

Discussion and Observation/Science Ideas

What do we use to taste with? Look at tongue in mirror. Can you see the taste buds? Talk about different tastes. Find the different taste areas on tongue. Try 'blindfold' tasting. Can you guess the taste? Can you taste with a dry tongue? Can you still taste things when you have a cold? Discuss the function of taste in the digestive process, and the pleasures/dangers of tasting.

Art and Craft

Food collage — use a variety of media to make a 'plate' of food.

Paint, draw or use collage ideas to make pictures of favourite/ least favourite foods.

Paintings or line drawings of expressions when licking ice cream/ eating cold cabbage etc.

Detailed drawings of tongue.

Maths

Make soup — weigh all ingredients carefully. Compare tastes of raw and cooked foods.

Taste tests — compare flavours of different orange drinks. Which is most popular? Why? Chart results.

Other Language Ideas

Vocabulary — sweet, sour, bitter, salty, delicious, scrumptious, disgusting, revolting, flavour, lick, saliva.

Expressions — 'good taste', 'no taste', 'tasting freedom', 'sweet as pie', 'sourpuss', 'bitterly', 'sweetly'.

Books and Stories

Thinkabout Tasting by Henry Pluckrose, Franklin Watts.
The Perfect Hamburger by A. McCall Smith, Young Puffin.

Poems and Rhymes

'A Matter of Taste' by Eve Merriam in *A Packet of Poems*, OUP.
'UCKG' by Michael Rosen in *A Packet of Poems*, OUP.

Songs and Music

'Sweet Things' in *Penny Whistles*, Blackie & Sons.
'Magical Food' in *Music Box Songbook*, BBC Enterprises Ltd.
'Horrid Tasting Things' in *Penny Whistles*, Blackie & Sons.

Display Board

Background — deep pink and white chequerboard, darker pink border. Letters of 'taste' — bright yellow on green. **Large 3D mouth** — see notes on 'Teeth'. **Tongue** — thin foam covered in pink tissue coated with PVA.

Display Table

Covered in white, pink and violet fabric. Sets of sweet/ salty things. Taste test — pots of sweet, sour, salty, bitter. Orange drinks.

Nose/Smell

Discussion and Observation/Science Ideas

What are your favourite/least favourite smells? Discuss smell associated with places — hospitals, schools, libraries, etc. Smell tests — blindfold a child who tries to identify various smells. Are there any smells that warn you of danger?

The smells of pollution. Everyday smells long ago — rotting piles of rubbish, sewage running through the streets. Use of pomanders, spices, posies of flowers and perfume by rich people to mask smells.

Art and Craft

Paint profiles.

Paint pictures of favourite/least favourite smells.

Pictures of places associated with smells — bakery, greengrocer, bookshop, garage, etc.

Maths

Graph of favourite/least favourite smell.

Record the smells that you can identify during one day.

Other Language Ideas

Vocabulary — fragrant, scent, perfume, aroma, odour, stink, stench.

Slang words for nose/smell — pong, sniff, whiff, pen and ink, hooter, conk.

Read 'An Episode of Noses' in *A Book of Bosh* by Edward Lear, Puffin, and make up own limericks.

Books and Stories

Smelling by Henry Pluckrose in 'Thinkabout' Series, Franklin Watts.

The Witch in the Cherry Tree by Margaret Mahy, Picture Puffin.

The Day the Smells Went Wrong by Catherine Sefton, 'Cartwheel' Series, Hamish Hamilton.

'The Elephant's Child' by Rudyard Kipling in *Just So Stories*, Piccolo.

Poems and Rhymes

'The Sniffle' by Ogden Nash in *Rhyme Time 2*, Beaver.

'Superstink' by Robert Froman in *Kingfisher Book of Children's Poetry*, Guild Publishing.

Songs & Music

'Wild and Wary' in *Mrs. Macaroni*, Macmillan Educational.

'Wrinkle up Your Nose' by Lesley Lees in *Jump into the Ring*, Ward Lock Educational.

Display Board

Background — green and white chequerboard, orange crêpe border. Letters of 'follow your nose' — red on black. Dustbin made out of foil-covered card.

Display Table

Covered in orange and yellow fabric. Provide a variety of things to smell — perfume, soap, bread, mint, spices, etc.

Writing

Discussion and Observation

What is writing? Look at examples of our own writing. Has it changed over the year? Why do we need to learn to write?

Writing as communication — long ago and now. Find examples in pictures, books and museums of writing from earliest days, including cave paintings and symbols, hieroglyphics, cuneiform, runes. What materials and tools were used?

Other languages — look at examples. How are they written? Can you see any similarities?

Look at the writing all around us — signs, symbols, labels, books, newspapers and magazines, letters, public buildings etc; different styles of writing, by hand and in print; codes; Pictograms.

Art and Craft

Make a cave painting — use crushed chalk, mixed with water, painted on to dark paper or stone, using brush made from a frayed twig; or use chalks, pastels on dark paper.

Design a label or advertisement. Use paint, felt-tips, oil pastels.

Look at examples of medieval illuminated letters. Draw and 'illuminate' initial letter of your own name — use fine felt-tips, metallic pens, coloured pencils, or crayons; fluorescent and metallic paints.

Torn newspaper pictures on black or contrasting colour.

Maths

Find the longest word you can. How many letters? How many words can you find with 2/3/4 letters?

Set up a Post Office corner. Include materials for activities such as addressing and weighing parcels, making stamps, matching cards to envelopes from a variety of shapes and sizes.

Look at collection times on post boxes. How long do First/Second class letters take to reach their destination? What times does your postman deliver your mail?

Writing

...The 🧙 sat on her 🧹 and flew away over the 🌙 and through the ⭐⭐⭐ until she reached the old 🌳...

Other Language Ideas

Vocabulary — 1) Historical — papyrus, parchment, stylus, quill, wax tablet, clay tablet, slate, ink, hieroglyphics, cuneiform, script, characters.

Vocabulary — 2) Names of different writing tools in use today.

What is Braille?

Development of printing, typewriters, word processors, Fax machines — will we need *hand* writing as a form of communication in the future?

Writing patterns.

Make own picture message or story (as illustrated).

Write a letter to a friend in another class.

Is it important to write neatly? Can you make your writing book look beautiful?

Learn how to write the word 'Welcome' in different languages.

What is a dictionary? Can you use one?

Have a 'Letter Food' party — with alphabet spaghetti, alphabet chips, chocolate biscuit letters. Can you make your own letter food?

Books and Stories

Sending Messages by Anne Mountfield in 'Looking Back At' Series, Macmillan Education Ltd.

Language and Writing by Miriam Moss, Wayland.

'How the First Letter was Written' by Rudyard Kipling, 'How the Alphabet was Made' by Rudyard Kipling, both from *Just So Stories*, Piccolo.

The Jolly Postman by Janet and Allan Ahlberg, William Heinemann Ltd.

Poems and Rhymes

'Windows' by Wes Magee in *Another Second Poetry Book*, OUP.

'Letters to Santa' by Jacqueline Brown in *Another First Poetry Book*, OUP.

'Playing with Words' by Michael Rosen in *The Kingfisher Book of Children's Poetry*, Guild Publishing.

Songs and Music

'The Ink is Black, the Page is White' in *Someone's Singing, Lord*, A & C Black.

'My First Week at School' in *Count Me In*, A & C Black.

'Postman Pat' by Brian Daly in *Children's Sunnyday Songbook*, International Music Publishers.

'I Sent a Letter', Trad. in *The Clarendon Book of Singing Games, Book II*, OUP.

Pictures to look at

'Posting the Letter', R.W. Chapman, 1857.

'Reading the Figaro', Mary Cassatt, 1883.

Display Board

Street scene as shown, built up in stages using mixed media. Border — children's brightly coloured and decorated letters, cut out and glued on to contrasting paper. Letters of 'writing' — black on fluorescent yellow paper banner. Attach banner to dowel rod — position in Postman Pat's van.

Display Table

Yellow fabric cover. 3D van made from boxes — toy Postman Pat inside. Hessian mailbag. School postbox. Books, including dual language stories, writing tools as illustrated. **Wax tablet** — melted candle wax poured into lid. **Clay tablet** — use Plasticine or slab of soft clay.

Birthdays

Can you guess what is in each parcel?

Discussion and Observation

When is your birthday? What month? How old are you?
What do you like best about having a birthday?
Names — why was your name chosen? What does it mean?
Special birthdays — 1st, 18th, 100th.
Compare photographs of children as babies. What changes have occurred?
Birthstones and flowers.
Zodiac signs. Do you know your sign?
How do children celebrate birthdays in other countries. Talk about different traditions and customs.
How did children celebrate birthdays long ago?
Who has had or been to a party recently? What games did you play? Did you wear special clothes?
Thinking of others — courtesy when receiving presents, during the party tea, on leaving a party; helping clear up; thoughtfulness towards a shy guest.

Art and Craft

Design a birthday banner — use brightly coloured or fluorescent paint, felt-tips or oil pastels.
Design and make birthday cards — use a variety of materials — paint, coloured pencils, crayons, wax resist technique, sequins, glitter, tissue, gummed paper, doilies.
Design and decorate a birthday cake — use a tin 'iced' with Polyfilla. Paint on design.
Make simple decorations — paper chains, lanterns, streamers.
Design and print gift wrapping — potato or carrot prints — cut potatoes and carrots into interesting shapes and print with bright colours on to good quality white paper (could colour wash the paper first).
Make table decorations — simple floral arrangements, or link with theme of party.

Maths

Weigh parcels — provide a variety of sizes and shapes.
Wrap presents — estimate how much paper/string needed.
Shape — make cone-shaped party hats.
Measure paper chains — whose is the longest/shortest? How many links on each? Make sequence pattern paper chains.
Make 'number' birthday cards.
Make chart showing in which month/season each child's birthday falls.
Days of the week — read 'Monday's Child', Trad. On which day were you born?
How much does your party food cost? **Visit** supermarket and write down prices.

Other Language Ideas

Make a wish when you blow out your birthday candles. Talk about wishes. Do we need to wish for something for ourselves all the time?
Make up a verse for a birthday card — read a selection first.
Describe your favourite party game. Make up own party games with a group of children.
Describe your last birthday, from your feelings on waking up in the morning, to clearing up at the end of the day.
Send invitations. Write thank you letters (from the guests).

Birthdays

Books and Stories

Birth Customs by John Mayled, Wayland.

Something Special for Me by Vera S. Williams, Walker Books.

Mister Rabbit and the Lovely Present, by Charlotte Zolotov/Maurice Sendak, Picture Puffin.

A Birthday for Frances by Russell Hoban, Hippo, Scholastic Publications.

Poems and Rhymes

'Happy Birthday Card' by Rony Robinson in *A Very First Poetry Book*, OUP.

'Waiting' by James Reeves in *The Oxford Treasury of Children's Poems*, Guild Publishing.

'The Hippopotamus' Birthday' by E.V. Rieu in *A Puffin Quartet of Poets.*

'The End' by A.A. Milne from *Now We are Six*, Methuen.

'Party Piece' by John Jenkins, in *A Very First Poetry Book*, OUP.

'Zodiac' by Eleanor Farjeon, in *The Oxford Treasury of Children's Verse*, Guild Publishing.

Songs and Music

'Happy Birthday to You', *Harlequin*, A & C Black.

'Come to the Party', *Game Songs from Prof. Dogg's Troupe*, A & C Black.

'How Old Are You?' from *Jump Into the Ring*, Ward Lock Educational.

'Sanjay's Party' from *Penny Whistles*, Contemporary Songs by Mike Moran, Blackie & Son Ltd.

Display Board

Wallpaper background — pale pink paper overprinted with darker pink flower shapes. Dark pink border. Children's own paintings of themselves dressed in party clothes, wearing hats, carrying party bags and balloons. Party table — fix cardboard to board, cover with paper cloth.

Display Table

Cover with bright cloth. Arrange party food, cards, presents, as shown.

Sleeping Beauty

Discussion and Observation

Read different versions of the story. Talk about the differences — number of fairies, names of the characters, the curse on the Princess, the arrival of the Prince. What did the Lilac Fairy do? What is lilac? If possible bring in some to look at and smell. Who has been to a christening and who has godparents? Why wasn't Carabosse invited? Invite local spinner to demonstrate spinning on a spinning-wheel. Where is the spindle? Have you ever seen a briar rose?

Listen to a recording of excerpts from Tchaikowsky's ballet.

Art and Craft

Individual collages of the Lilac Fairy and Carabosse.

Use plenty of glitter, sequins, net, shiny and metallic fabrics and papers to achieve a magical effect, in shades of black/grey/silver for Carabosse and pink/lilac/white/gold for the Lilac Fairy.

Faces — draw an angry or frightening face; a peaceful, pleasant face. (Practise making faces in the mirror!)

'Aurora' means dawn — talk about sunrise and sunset. Make pictures of both. (Look at 'Impression, Sunrise', Monet, 1873, and 'Poplars on the Epte, Sunset', Monet, 1891.)

Look at design of medieval castles. How were they constructed? What building materials were used? Make models of castles, individually or in groups. Would you be safe in your castle? Does the drawbridge work?

Maths

Work with 100's.

Research local area and find out how it has changed over the last century — visit libraries, talk to old people to find out what the area was like when they were younger.

Make stars for wands, with five, six or eight points. Can you make a 3, 4, or 7 pointed star?

Other Language Ideas

Write story of the Sleeping Beauty in own words.

Descriptive writing comparing the evil Carabosse with the good, kind Lilac Fairy.

Vocabulary — feast, ceremony, preparation, invitation, beauty, wisdom, grace, curse, distaff, celebrate, enchantment, courtier, scullion, spit.

Design and send invitations to another class, inviting them to join in wedding celebrations of Princess Aurora and Prince Florimund. Choose Prince and Princess. Children could wear party or dressing-up clothes, and sing appropriate songs. Hold 'wedding feast' and play appropriate excerpts from Tchaikowsky's ballet.

Life in a medieval castle.

Sleeping Beauty

How many hours' sleep do you have each night?

Books and Stories

'The Sleeping Beauty', retold by Catherine Storr, *Easy Piano Picture Book*, Faber and Faber.

The Sleeping Beauty, retold by Josephine Poole, Hutchinson Children's Books Ltd.

The Sleeping Beauty, Francesca Crespa, Hodder and Stoughton.

Life in a Castle, by Althea, Cambridge University Press.

Songs and Music

'The Princess', in *Okki Tokki Unga*, A & C Black.

The Sleeping Beauty', in *The Clarendon Book of Singing Games, Book 1*, Herbert Wiseman and Sydney Northcote, OUP.

'Briar Rosebud', in *The Clarendon Book of Singing Games Book 2*, OUP.

Excerpts from Tchaikowsky's ballet, 'The Sleeping Beauty'.

Display Board

Large picture of the Prince waking Aurora. Above board — castle turrets painted in shades of grey. Overprint in white with large plastic brick or box lid for stone block or brick pattern. Coat with PVA when dry.

Towers — Paint and print card as above. Coat with PVA and sprinkle with silver glitter. Bend into a long tube shape. Make cone shapes large enough to overlap top of tower by a few inches. Cover cones with foil. Attach towers to board at top and bottom by stapling inside tube. Flatten cone slightly at back to fit tower. Attach to tower with masking tape under overlapping edge. Secure back of cone to board.

Briars — Twisted brown crêpe paper or fabric. Drape round tower and at top of board. Secure with staples.

Leaves — Cut from paper/fabric/foil in shades of green. Attach to briars and towers. Paint flowers pink with yellow centres and coat with PVA. Drape silver lametta round briars.

Characters — Paint faces and hands; coat with PVA. 'Dress' with paper, fabric and other collage materials.

Lilac Fairy — shades of lilac and silver. Use shiny fabrics, with net or chiffon, sequins, glitter and silver doilies. Silver foil wings sprinkled with glitter.

Florimund — Shiny fabrics in shades of red or purple.

Carabosse — Green face, deeper green hair, sprinkled with green glitter. Glue on a few strands of green lametta. Black cloak and hat.

Aurora — white dress with gold sequins or doilies at neckline. Gold foil coronet.

Bedspread, pillow and bed — shades of pink fabric trimmed with gold doily edging. Gold bed frame.

Writing at sides of board: on pale pink paper edged with gold doilies.

Display Table

Deep red fabric cover. Children's dolls and teddy bears in medieval costume, as shown. Spinning wheel if available. Drape narrow strips of silver lametta, white net or similar, to give a 'cobweb' effect. Books and stories. Book of children's writing.

Music

Discussion and Observation/ Music Ideas

Ask the children what they think music is. Why do we make music? What sorts of music are there? Play short taped examples. Which did they like best, and why?

Different instruments and their music — in pictures, at museums, or best of all, hearing and seeing them played.

Music for many occasions — seasonal and religious festivals, military, weddings, country dances.

Music in history — look at development of music from earliest times. What were the instruments made from? How did they work? What did they look like? What sounds did they make? Invite an Early Music group to play for the children.

Listen to music from different countries. Discuss similarities and differences. Arrange a musical event incorporating music, song and dance from around the world.

Use variety of everyday objects — paper, foil, bottles, tins, lids, wood — to explore ways of making musical sounds. Combine with other instruments, tuned and untuned percussion — either to make music as an accompaniment for a song or story or to create a simple piece of group/class music, starting from basic rhythms and ideas. Use children's own symbols to record class or individual compositions.

Art and Craft

Make instruments using lengths of metal tubing, wood, glass paper, cans, and other everyday materials. Can we make tuned instruments? How?

Draw individual instruments from observation, perhaps being played. Use soft pencils, Conté crayon, charcoal, fine felt-tipped pens or oil pastels, on white cartridge paper.

Fabric/paper collages, or paintings, of children dancing, singing or playing instruments.

Print instruments using appropriate shapes — boxes, lids, card edges, yoghurt pots, drinking straws.

Read story and listen to some of the music of a well-known ballet. Paint favourite scene, using large sheet of paper and beginning with the background. Add small details with collage materials.

Maths

'Shape pictures' of instruments.

Counting/clapping/playing in time to rhythms.

Note value — minim, crotchet, quaver.

Number rhymes and songs.

Vocabulary — trio, quartet, quintet, sextet.

Music

This is me Playing my favourite instrument — a recorder

Other Language Activities

Vocabulary — treble clef, bass clef, note, rhythm, bar, rest, stave; opera, symphony orchestra, composer, conductor, scene, overture, finale; gentle, soft, lively, loud, slow, sad, flowing.

Musical expressions: 'He who pays the piper calls the tune', 'dance to a different tune', 'music to my ears', 'I'll lead you a merry dance'.

Write about a short piece of music. Did you like it? What instruments could you hear? Was it happy or sad, slow or fast, loud or soft?

Other Ideas

Arrange **visit** to schools' concert or invite group of musicians to school, including any willing volunteer parents, friends or siblings.

Organise music workshops for parents only, or for parents and children in a class, making music together or making instruments.

Books and Stories

Trubloff: The Mouse Who Wanted to Play the Balalaika, by John Burningham, Jonathan Cape Ltd.

Our Steel Band, by Rachel Warner, Hamish Hamilton Children's Books.

Musical Instruments, by Alan Blackwood, Wayland.

Mr. Bear the Drummer, by Chizuko Kuratomi, Macdonald.

Making Musical Instruments, Macmillan Publishers Ltd.

Poems and Rhymes

'The Ceremonial Band', by James Reeves, in *Poems for 9 Year Olds*, Puffin.

'The Parade' in *What a Wonderful Day*, chosen by Tony Bradman, Blackie.

'Flute Girl', by Roderick Hunt, in *A First Poetry Book*, OUP.

Songs and Music

'Would you Like to Sing a Song?' by Jane Sebba in *Playalong Songs,* Hamish Hamilton.

'The Percussion Family' by Brenda Piper, in *Sing as you Grow*, Ward Lock Educational.

'Over the Hills and Far Away', Trad.

Songs from *A Musical Calendar of Festivals*, Ward Lock.

Songs from *The Music Box Songbook*, BBC Books.

Pictures to look at

'The Guitarist', Monet, 1860.

'Café Singer', Edgar Degas, 1878.

'A Young Woman Seated at a Virginal', Johannes Vermeer, 1670.

Display Board

Background — any bright colour. Border — cut notes from card. Letters of 'making music' — white on black paper. Children's pictures backed in black on contrasting colour.

Display Table

Cover to match board, terraced with boxes. Display of folk and other instruments. Chime bars. Rhythm cards. Paper and pencils to write own rhythms or tunes. Children's home-made instruments. Books and stories.

The Moon

Discussion and Observation/Science Ideas

Read 'Silver' by Walter de la Mare, in *The Book of a Thousand Poems.* Have you seen the moon? Is it always in the same place? Is the colour/shape always the same? What makes the moon shine? Is the moon really made of green cheese? Have you seen the man in the moon? How would we get to the moon? How long would it take? Talk about the first lunar landing. How did the astronauts travel to the moon? What special equipment and clothing did they need, and why? What is gravity? What would happen if you tried to drink a glass of milk or eat a school dinner on the moon? Find out about the pull of the moon on the earth. What effect does it have on the oceans?

Art and Craft

Texture — is the moon smooth? Look at photographs and pictures of the moon.

Textured moon pictures — on heavy paper or thin card. Suggest moon surface, craters and mountains, using variety of junk materials such as polystyrene packing, sections of egg boxes, lids, bottle tops of different sizes, sand. Either paint with suitable 'moon' coloured thick paint (coat with PVA when dry), cover with silver foil or spray silver. Add glitter as required.

Paint or use collage technique for 'man in the moon' pictures.

Make 3D moons out of balloons covered with papier mâché. Paint when dry.

Design and make a moving moon buggy out of junk materials, Lego or other construction toys.

Pasta moons — sprayed silver and sprinkled with glitter.

Maths

Shape — crescent, half moon, gibbous moon, full moon — line drawings or cut out of gummed paper.

Time — night and day, seasons. How long does the moon take to complete all its phases?

Other Language Ideas

Vocabulary — lunar, gravity, atmosphere, orbit, surface, craters, countdown, astronaut, meteorites, wax, wane. After reading a collection of 'moon' stories, discuss which the children liked best, and why.

Read *Whatever Next,* and the rhyme 'There was an old woman went up in a basket'. Can you really travel to the moon in a cardboard box or basket? Why not?

Movement/Drama

Listen to 'Claire de Lune'. Discuss ways of moving with the music.

Books and Stories

Whatever Next by Jill Murphy, Picture Mac.
I want to see the moon by Louis Baum, Magnet, Methuen Children's Books.
Going to the moon by Brenda Williams, in 'Stepping Stones' Series, Kingfisher.

Poems and Rhymes

'Humpty Dumpty went to the moon' by Michael Rosen, *A Very First Poetry Book,* OUP.
'Silver' by Walter de la Mare, in *The Book of a Thousand Poems,* Bell & Hyman.
'Bedtime' in *Lullabies,* illustrated by Hilda Offen, Kingfisher Books Ltd.

Songs and Music

'Aiken Drum', Trad.
'The Moon Song', *Sixty Songs for Little Children,* OUP.

The Moon

Pictures to look at

'The Starry Night', Van Gogh, 1889.
'Shields Lighthouse', J.M.W. Turner, c.1826.

AIKEN DRUM

Display Board

Background — dark blue, silver foil stars. Letters of 'Aiken Drum' — silver foil glued on card and cut out. Aiken Drum's **crescent moon** — painted yellow. **Aiken Drum** — top half of body cut out of card (slices of roast beef) — textured reddish-brown fabric; **waistcoat** (crust of pies) — painted in shades of light brown; **buttons** (penny loaves) — small loaf shapes cut out of foam and painted brown; **hat** — old hat covered in thick, cream-coloured fabric. Cut edge of fabric to resemble melting cheese as shown. **Trousers** (haggis bags) — stuff tights with plenty of newspaper until the legs are fat. Fasten brown fabric around each of his legs and dab fabric with paint in shades of brown. Cover with Clingfilm. Cut card feet and staple to end of legs — cover with socks. **Ladle** — cut out of card covered with silver foil, or use large catering ladle. **Man in the Moon** (middle) — painted yellow. **Man in the Moon** (right) — painted with pale cream paint sprinkled with glitter. **Arms and legs** — pale green. **Shoes** — silver foil. Children's individual pictures backed in yellow or silver foil. **Cobwebs** — silver lametta.

Display Table

Fabric to match board. Make roast beef, cream cheese, penny loaves, crust of pies, haggis, out of dough, papier mâché or clay. **Old woman in basket** — dressed doll; make small birch broom. **Cold pease porridge** — mix thick wallpaper paste. Add food colouring. **Cow jumping over moon** — cut two identical shapes from card. Paint each, then glue two matchboxes between each shape so that model is self-supporting. Toy owl and pussycat. Rhymes on cards. Book of children's favourite moon rhymes.

THE MOON

Display Board

Black background — letters of 'the moon' cut out from card covered with silver foil. Large moon made by glueing junk materials on to large circle of card or thick paper, and spraying with silver paint.

Display Table

White/blue shiny and silver fabric. Scene from *Whatever Next* — large cardboard box, teddy, boots, space helmet, toys etc. Books and stories.

Up in the Air

Discussion and Observation/Science Ideas

Go outside. What can you see up in the air? Clouds, seeds, insects, birds, aeroplanes, gliders, balloons, kites, helicopters. Discuss how they get up in the air. Has anyone even been up in the air? Compare things that move through the air with those that float in the air. Discuss the effects of wind on flight. Visit relevant museum or airport.

Maths/Science Activities

Count and record the number of airborne things you see during one day.

Make a kite — experiment with different shapes and materials. Measure tails of kites. Order according to length.

Art and Craft

Wax resist pictures of things that go up in the air — crayon thickly first and cover with pale blue wash.

Make hot air balloons — net fruit bags over balloons tied to decorated margarine tubs.

Gaily decorated kites — use lots of thick, brightly coloured or fluorescent paint; tinsel or lametta streamers.

Junk models of birds, butterflies and flying insects.

Hot air balloon pictures: background — sponge-printed sky, brightly painted/collage balloon.

Other Language Ideas

Vocabulary — soaring, gliding, hovering, fluttering, swooping, diving, lift, take-off, flight paths, runway, propeller, jet engines.

Use poem as starting point for creative writing e.g. 'The Swing', *Happy Landings.*

Musical Activities

Make up rhythm patterns using flight words such as aeroplane, glider, helicopter, bee. Use combinations of body or untuned percussion.

Movement

Discuss different ways of moving through the air. Listen to the 'Flight of the Bumblebee' and use music as a basis for movement.

Books and Stories

Kites and Gliders in 'Starters Science', Macdonald, *Balloons,* Macdonald Starters.

Kit and the Magic Kite by Helen Cooper, Picture Corgi, Hamish Hamilton Children's Books.

Up and Up by Shirley Hughes, Picture Lion.

Poems and Rhymes

'The Kite' by Pearl Forbes MacEwan in *The Book of a Thousand Poems,* Bell & Hyman.

'The Swing' by Robert Louis Stevenson in *Happy Landings,* Evan Bros. Ltd.

Songs & Music

'My beautiful balloon', in *Mrs. Macaroni,* Macmillan Educational.

'Flight of the Bumblebee', Rimsky-Korsakov.

Display Board

Pale blue background, darker blue border. Letters of 'up in the air' cut out of spare sponge-printed paper, backed with darker blue.

Display Table

Dark blue shiny fabric; stiff white net for cloud effect. Junk models of insects, birds, aeroplanes, toy aeroplanes, helicopters etc.

Dragons

Discussion and Observation

Read a selection of dragon legends — Tiamat the Babylonian Dragon, Chinese Dragons, Japanese Dragons, Jason and the Golden Fleece, St. George and the Dragon. What do dragons look like in stories and legends? Where did they live? Were they fierce or friendly? Do you believe in dragons? What do *you* think they look like? Discuss the influence of the word 'dragon' during the Middle Ages, e.g. a chief was called a dragon because he was fierce. Find out about Uther Pendragon. Why was a musket called a 'dragoon'? Why were dragons so important in Chinese culture? Look at examples of Chinese art and architecture. Find out about Komodo dragons.

Art and Craft

Pictures of dragons using thick, brightly coloured and fluorescent paint. Add coloured foils, egg box sections, collage materials, glitter, glitter stars.

Junk models.

Look at illustrations of dragons. Discuss size, colour, shape. Draw your favourite dragon on good quality white paper using pencils, felt-tips, oil pastels.

Look at other dragons and paint pictures of Welsh dragons, Chinese dragons, Perseus and Andromeda.

Clay, dough or Plasticine models.

Maths

Make a 'shape' dragon, either 2D or 3D. Which shapes have you used?

How many scales can you fit on your dragon? — use pre-cut circles of green papers.

Other Language Ideas

Vocabulary — fiery, fierce, flaming, nostrils, scales. Write own dragon story.

Books and Stories

The Dragon's Cold by John Talbot, Walker Books.
There's No Such Thing as a Dragon by Jack Kent, Blackie.
St. George and the Dragon retold by Margaret Hodges, Little, Brown & Co.
Lizards and Dragons by Lionel Bender in 'Sight' Series, Franklin Watts.

Poems and Rhymes

'The Lonely Dragon' by Theresa Heine in *Another First Poetry Book,* OUP.
'Dragon Night' by Jane Yolen, *Oxford Treasury of Children's Poems,* Guild Publishing.

Songs and Music

'Puff the Magic Dragon' in *Sing a Song One,* Thomas Nelson & Sons.

Pictures to look at

'St. George and the Dragon', Moreau.
'St. George and the Dragon', Tintoretto.

Display Board

Background — orange and yellow chequerboard, orange border. Letters of 'dragons' — green foil on gold.

Display Table

Covered in orange, red and yellow fabric. Junk and clay models of dragons.

The Legend of Persephone

Discussion and Observation

Read the legend of Persephone. Discuss the changing seasons in relation to the story. Why was Demeter sad? What did she do? How do you think Persephone felt when she was carried off by Pluto? Bring in a pomegranate. Cut it open, look at seeds and taste. Find out where and how pomegranates grow.

Art and Craft

Pomegranates — draw from observation — whole fruit or half. Use fine felt-tip pens for outlines, wider felt-tips for filling in and shading, or use wax crayons or oil pastels.

Fabric collages — select appropriate shades in smooth shiny fabrics.

Individual pictures of scenes from the story.

Colour exercise — fold white paper into large squares or rectangles. Discuss the colours that the children associate with each season. Allow each child to pick a season, then paint each square in a different shade of chosen colours. Demonstrate how to vary shades by addition of small amounts of other colours, or black/white. Look at finished pictures with the children. How different are the children's interpretations of each season?

Paint pictures of favourite season.

Maths/Science Ideas

Time — months of year; seasonal changes. Activities in the farming year — ploughing, sowing, haymaking, harvesting.

Look closely at pomegranate. Cut into halves, quarters, slices. Observe any pattern or symmetry. Look at structure of fruit.

Other Language Activities

Other fruits beginning with 'P'.

How many words can be made using the letters in 'pomegranate'?

Choose a season. Which words or phrases describe it best?

Music and Drama Activities

Mime story accompanied with tuned and untuned percussion or use everyday objects to create mood music to set the scene.

Books and Stories

The Changing Seasons, 'Science Starters' Series, Franklin Watts.

Spring by David Lambert
Summer by Ralph Whitlock
Autumn by Ralph Whitlock
Winter by David Lambert, Wayland.

Song to Demeter by Cynthia and William Birrer, Julia Macrae.

'Persephone' in *Stories for Seven Year Olds,* Puffin.

The Legend of Persephone

Demeter is upset because her daughter, Persephone, has been taken away by Pluto.

Poems and Rhymes

'Spring Song' by Jean Kenward in *A Very First Poetry Book,* OUP.

'Summer Song' by John Ciardi in *The Book of a Thousand Poems,* Bell & Hyman.

'Autumn' by Florence Hoatson in *The Book of a Thousand Poems,* Bell & Hyman.

'Winter Morning' by Ogden Nash in *A First Poetry Book,* OUP.

'Pluto and Proserpine' by James Reeves in *The Wandering Moon and Other Poems,* Puffin.

Songs and Music

'The Four Seasons' by Vivaldi.

'Look for Signs That Summer's Done' in *Someone's Singing, Lord,* A. & C. Black.

Pictures to look at

'The Return of Persephone' Lord Leighton of Stretton, 1891 (City of Leeds Art Gallery).

'The Abduction of Proserpine' Rembrandt.

Display Board

Back left-hand side in orange; right-hand side in green. Letters of 'Persephone' — yellow paper backed with dark brown. Border — gold foil.

Pluto — draw on paper, cut out and dress with paint and fabric or paper collage. Robe — purple, sprinkled with silver glitter. Grey hair and beard, silver foil crown.

Autumn leaves — cut out leaf prints, or leaf shapes from gold and red foil, and papers in red, orange or yellow.

Demeter — robe — shades of yellow.

Garland of fruit — use string, paper leaves and plastic fruit to make garland. Attach ends to board with staples. Children's pictures backed in dark brown or black with yellow.

Display Table

Fabric to match board. **Pluto's side** — make 3D figure of Persephone using tights stuffed with newspaper or polystyrene. Cut hands and feet from card, paint and staple to ends of arms and legs. 'Dress' figure in old dress or drape with fabric, cutting or stapling where necessary to fit figure. Cut head shape out of card, paint and staple in place on body and on board to hold in place. Gold foil crown. Paint and cut out pomegranate from card; staple to hand or attach with sticky tape.

Vases of autumn foliage; bundles of dried grasses; twigs, seedheads or dried flowers. Cotton squares with children's autumn leaf print design.

Demeter's side — dish of real fruits, or make from papier mâché, clay or dough, painted and varnished. Spring or summer flowers. Pomegranates. Fabric with fruit design — or use one with a Spring or Summer theme. Books of children's writing.

3D Pomegranate — make papier mâché shell around large balloon. When dry, cut in half. Paint and coat with PVA. Stuff shell with newspaper. Cut stiff card to fit inside rim of shell. Glue on egg-box sections. Paint bright red and coat with PVA. Sprinkle with red glitter.

Water

I like splashing in the bath.

What do you like doing in the bath?

Discussion and Observation/Science Ideas

Describe water and its properties. Discuss liquids. Why do living things need water? Talk about drought and its effects on communities in the Third World and attempts to remedy the situation.

Discuss the uses of water at home, in industry, farming and the community at large.

Where does water come from? Draw the water cycle — rain, condensation, evaporation.

Science Activities

Set up simple experiments to show evaporation and condensation.

Observe the effects of freezing, thawing and heating on water.

Show how plants absorb water through stem by placing flowers (daffodils, carnations or celery) in jars of coloured water. Ask children beforehand what they think will happen.

Wet and dry — explore properties of sand, soil and of a variety of fabrics.

Reflections in water.

Dehydrated food — soak to see what happens.

Maths

Water tray — provide transparent plastic tubing, funnels, sieves, water wheels, spoons etc. for floating and sinking.

Capacity work: vocabulary — full, empty, half full, pints, litres, half litres. Filling and emptying containers of differing size and shape; conservation of volume.

Art and Craft

Marbling — shades of blue/green/white. Could use as a background for collage work.

'Wet paper' pictures — drop paint or coloured inks on to wet paper. When dry coat with PVA.

Drop a pebble into a large bowl of water. Observe patterns of concentric ripples. Paint observations on round white paper in shades of blue (see display board).

Other Language Ideas

Vocabulary — splash, gush, trickle, torrent, ooze, drip, damp, soaked, drenched, wet.

'Water is . . .' How many ways can you describe water?

Use a poem as a starting point for class/group discussion, perhaps leading to creative writing.

Musical Activities

Watery sounds — what different sounds can be made with water?

Fill glass bottles with different levels of water and tap gently with beater. Arrange in sequence of lowest to highest sound.

Cooking Activities

Which drinks are made with water?

Investigate ways of cooking with water.

Water

Books and Stories

Water, Macdonald First Library.

Looking at Water by Jo Sowry, Batsford Educational.

Children Need Water by Wendy Davies, Wayland.

'The Flying Water' by Leila Berg, in *Time for one more,* Magnet.

Andrew's Bath, David McPhail, Picture Puffin.

Come away from the water, Shirley by John Burningham, Collins.

Splash! All about baths by Susan Kovacs Buxbaum and Rita Golden Gelman, Hodder & Stoughton.

Poems and Rhymes

'Sound of Water' by Mary O'Neill, in *Singing in the Sun,* Young Puffin.

'Water' by John R. Gossland, in *A Book of a Thousand Poems,* Bell & Hyman.

'Water when you're thirsty' by Clive Riche in *Is a Caterpillar Ticklish?* Young Puffin.

'The Plughole man' by Carey Blyton, *A Second Poetry Book,* OUP.

Songs and Music

'Glug glug glug' in *Mrs Macaroni* by June Tillman, Macmillan Educational.

'Underwater' in *Mrs. Macaroni* by June Tillman, Macmillan Educational.

'Marching in our wellingtons', by June Tillman, *Kokoleoko,* Macmillan.

'Raindrop prelude' for piano, Chopin.

Pictures to look at

'Water lilies', Monet, 1899.

'The Banks of the Marne at Chennevières', by Pissaro, 1864-5.

'Portrait of an Artist' (Pool with two figures), David Hockney.

Display Board

Pale blue background, darker blue border. Letters of 'water' cut out of left-over marbling pictures, as illustrated. Children's individual pictures backed in white and blue as appropriate.

Display Table

Royal blue/pale blue shiny fabric with white net draped to resemble waves. Floating and sinking tank, toy boats, ducks, windsurfers etc. Books and stories. Book of children's writing.

Noah's Ark

Discussion and Observation/Science Ideas

Read or tell the story of Noah's Ark. Discuss the story. Why did God send a flood? What is a flood? Flood disasters — why do they happen? What are the dangers to the survivors? Can floods be prevented? Why did God save Noah and his family? Why were there two of each animal saved? Talk about baby animals.

Why did God put a rainbow in the sky? What is a rainbow? Can we make our own? What is an ark? What wood did Noah use to make it? How did he make it watertight? Can we make our arks watertight?

Other Science Activities

Floating and sinking. Displacement of water. The weather: measuring rainfall. Make weather charts with symbols drawn by the children. Temperature changes during the day.

Art and Craft

Individual pictures of different scenes from the story. Background first: **grass** — print with sponge and card edges; **sky** — sponge or roller-print; **rain** — silver lametta, or glue lines of silver glitter; **sea** — apply thick paint in greys and blues, twist and roll cotton reel through it for stormy waves; **ark** — brown wood-effect paper, bark rubbings on brown paper using brown or black crayons. Draw and paint **animals** — glue on.

'After the flood' pictures — **sky** — circle print with yoghurt pots in shades of blue. **Grass** as before. **Rainbow** — oil pastels, felt-tips or paint — cut out separately and glue on. Make bread/fruit/cheese using clay, papier mâché or dough. Make model arks and animals from junk materials and fabrics.

Maths

Counting in twos.

Sets of two objects.

Sharing — how much bread/cheese/fruit is needed for eight people? Make a picnic lunch.

Weighing/balancing food needed.

Measuring in cubits.

Time — how many days and nights was Noah's family on the ark? How many weeks?

Other Language Ideas

Names of animals — classify into groups of mammals, birds, reptiles etc.

Unscrambling jumbled animal names.

What would you pack in your bag if you were going on board the ark?

Make a book about a favourite animal, using school reference library for information.

Make an alphabet zoo.

Noah's Ark

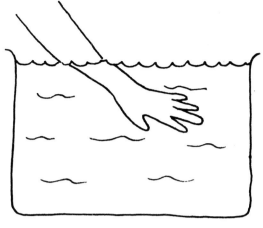

Look down at your arm. What can you see?

What happens to the water level?

Books and Stories

Noah's Brother by Dick King-Smith, Victor Gollancz.
Noah and His Ark retold by Catherine Storr, Franklin Watts.
Trouble in the Ark by Gerald Rose, The Bodley Head.

Poems and Rhymes

'The Prayer of the Little Ducks Who Went in the Ark' Trans. by Rumer Godden, *Junior Voices I,* Penguin.
'Noah' by Gerda Mayer in *The Oxford Treasury of Children's Poems,* Guild Publishing.
'Noah' by James Reeves in *The Oxford Treasury of Children's Poems,* Guild Publishing.
'The History of the Flood' by John Heath-Stubbs in *All Along Down Along,* a book of stories in verse, Longman Young Books.

Songs and Music

'The Animals Went in Two by Two', *Appuskidu,* A & C Black.
'Who Built the Ark?' in *Someone's Singing, Lord,* A & C Black.
'One More River', *Oxford Nursery Book, OUP.*

Picture to look at

'The Return of the Dove to the Ark', Sir John Everett Millais, 1851.

Display Board

Sky — roller print in shades of pale blue. **Sea** — comb prints — mix thick green/blue paint. Spread on sheet of plastic or glass. Comb in to wave pattern with stiff card 'comb'. Place sheet of paper onto paint; rub lightly with palm. Peel off and allow to dry. Repeat as necessary. Splatter print with white paint using toothbrush for 'sea spray'.
The Ark — paint corrugated cardboard; overprint in darker brown with small sponge. Coat with P.V.A. when dry. **Ark house** — light brown painted walls; or use brown corduroy fabric. **Animals and characters** — appropriate fabrics, paper collage, oil pastels, crayon. **Rainbow** — cut narrow, curved strips of paper, one for each colour of the rainbow. Decorate each in a variety of ways — fabrics, papers, foils, sequins, buttons or paints. Coat with PVA; decorate with glitter here and there. Repeat with other half of rainbow. Staple to board as shown.
Letters of 'Noah's Ark' — paint white paper with rainbow stripes. Cut out letters. Back with gold foil. **Rain** — silver foil 'drops'; short strips of silver lametta. **Sun** — paper collage in bright yellow or cut from gold foil. **Border** — cut leaves from a variety of green papers.

Display Table

Green fabric cover — dye old candlewick bedspread for grassy texture. Ark model from junk materials. Toy animals; children's own animal models. Fruit, bread and cheese from dough or clay, hardened, painted and varnished. Pots and jars — make from clay or paint old containers to resemble ancient pots. Rough textured fabrics for sheet and blanket. Hay and straw in wicker basket. Books, stories, book of children's writing.

Drama

Improvise story with no props. Discuss what God might have said to Noah.

Rocks and Stones

Discussions and Observation/Science Ideas

Read and discuss the poem 'Stones by the Sea'. Who has been on a pebbly beach? What did the pebbles feel like under your feet? Where else can you find rocks, stones, pebbles? Go outside. How many different stones can you find? Make a collection of rocks and stones, label with place found and examine with a viewer/magnifying glass. Look at colour, shape, pattern, texture, structure. Is the stone the same all over? Does it bounce, roll, slide? Why do some roll better than others?

Carry out 'hardness tests' on rocks. Scratch surface with fingernails, coin, screwdriver, other stones. Use vice to hold rock still. Record results.

What is a fossil? Can you see any in your samples? **Visit** museum to look at rocks, minerals and fossils. Can you identify your samples? What other things are found underground in the rocks?

Uses of rock and stone in building, both functional and decorative. Which types of stone are most suitable for building?

Concrete and bricks — are they rocks?

How are rocks formed?

Look at samples of clay and sand. How are they formed?

Art and Craft

Drawing from observation — natural patterns, markings, colours in stones and in stone/brick buildings. Use pencils, pastels, oil pastels or Conté crayons.

Paint design on large stone, slate or pebble — varnish when dry.

Make mosaic design using tiny stones — arrange in plaster of Paris in small suitable frame (e.g. a lid). Varnish when dry; or arrange design on card, glued with thick layer of PVA.

Look at museum exhibits of clay pots and make own. Do your pots hold liquids? How can they be made waterproof?

Make a 'stone' from clay. Paint and varnish when dry.

Make stone/brick rubbings on white paper.

Maths

Ordering — put stones in order of weight, estimate first, then weigh in grammes.

Use different grades of pebbles, grit, stone chippings and sand for work with capacity, volume, weighing and balancing activities.

Rocks and Stones

Read "Stone Soup" by Tony Ross.
Can you find a stone and
make some delicious soup?

Scrub your
stone
clean first!

Does it work?

Other Language Ideas

Vocabulary — types of rocks, stones, minerals; earthquake, volcano, ore, glacier, earth's crust.

Find out about jobs and hobbies associated with rocks and stone.

How and when did Stone Age people live? Why are they so called? Visit museum.

Expressions — 'heart of stone', 'stony-faced', 'blood out of a stone', 'a rolling stone gathers no moss', 'plenty more pebbles on the beach'.

Creative writing — imagine you are a pebble on the beach — write about what happens in your day.

Read 'The Inchcape Rock'. Discuss poem and re-tell in own words.

Cooking — make rock cakes!

Other Ideas

Plan rock garden design on paper, including suitable plants. Make small rock garden in school grounds/trough. **Visit** garden centre to buy materials and plants.

Books and Stories

Stone Soup by Tony Ross, Beaver Books, Arrow Books Ltd.

'The Crow & the Pitcher' (Aesop's Fables) retold by Joseph Jacobs in *The Puffin Children's Treasury.*

The Hill and the Rock by David McKee, Beaver Books, Arrow Books Ltd.

The Story of David and Goliath.

Rock Collecting by Roma Gans, 'First Sight' Series, A & C Black.

Rocks, Minerals and Fossils, by Mark C. W. Sleep, Wayland.

Poems and Rhymes

'Stony' by Eric Finney in *Another First Poetry Book,* OUP.

'The Inchcape Rock' by Robert Southey in *The Golden Treasury of Poetry,* selected by Louis Untermeyer, Collins.

'Walls' by Jean Kenward in *Another First Poetry Book,* OUP.

'Pebbles' by Leonard Clark in *Four Seasons,* Dobson Books Ltd.

'Stones by the Sea' by James Reeves in *A Puffin Quartet of Poets.*

Songs and Music

'Rocky Land' by Douglas Coombes in *Trig Trog,* 50 Songs from School Broadcasts, OUP.

'Only a Boy Named David' by A. S. Arnott in *Count Me In,* A & C Black.

'The Wise Man and the Foolish Man' in *Okki-Tokki-Unga,* A & C Black.

'Fossils' — 'Carnival of the Animals' by Saint Saëns.

Pictures

Find pictures of famous stone constructions and buildings throughout the world; also interesting natural rock formations.

Display Board

Background — bright pink/white chequerboard. Border of 'rocks' — sponge print paper in shades of brown and grey; when dry, spray on white or grey paint using old toothbrush. Finally, crumple the paper lightly and staple on edges of board, padding with newspaper at intervals. Letters of 'Rocks and Stones' — silver foil on black. **Rock climber** — 'dress' figure in paint or fabric/paper collage. Use thick string for rope. **Cave** — black paper stapled to board; rock borders as before. Children's pictures backed in black and appropriate contrasting colour.

Display Table

Bright pink cover. Samples of rocks, stones, crystals, fossils. Tools — geologist's hammer, chisels, sieve, stiff brush. Bowl of clay covered with damp cloth; board and tools for working with clay. Children's pots and painted stones. Dolls, dressed as cave dwellers in fur fabric. Attach pieces of flint to dolls' hands for tools. Twigs and Cellophane 'flames'. Book of children's writing. Books and stories.

Earth

Discussion and Observation/Science Ideas

Bring in large bowl of earth. Feel it. Smell it. What is it? What other names do we use? Where do we find earth? Look at different samples of earth. What do they feel like? Are the colours different? Spread each sample on to white plate or card. What can you see in each sample? Try to identify soil types — chalky, sandy, clay, loam. Grow same plants in different soil types. Observe and record results.

Mix each sample in separate jars of water till blended. Allow to settle undisturbed on windowsill. How does each settle? Are there any distinct layers? Which sample has most sand/stones/clay?

Visit local park/woodland/nature reserve. Select small area about 1 metre square. Observe animal life, grasses, flowers, mosses etc. Record findings in writing or in careful line drawings — use magnifying glass or viewer to study patterns, markings, colour and shape.

Find out about animals/minibeasts which live underground.

Art and Craft

Earth pictures — cover card with thick layer of PVA. Sprinkle on soils of different colours to make pattern.

'Ground level' pictures: **Earth** — sponge print, or use pile or rough-weave fabrics in shades of brown. **Sky** — roller-print in shades of blue. **Grass, flowers, insects, minibeasts** — use mixed media of printing/collage of grasses, seeds, pulses, feathers, tiny stones/grit, straw, twigs, paper.

The farming year — make pictures of different stages of crop farming — ploughing, furrowing, sowing, harvesting; or working the soil with hand tools in garden or allotment. Use paint, crayons, oil pastels, ordinary pastels.

Maths

Weigh different types of soil e.g. 1 cup of sandy soil weighs – g. Repeat with clay/chalk/peat soils. Which is heaviest/lightest?

Count number of insects or minibeasts in 1 square metre of soil.

How much water is there in your soil samples? Collect cupfuls of soil after it has rained. Weigh soil and record. Allow sample to dry out. Weigh again. Note any weight difference. Which soils do you think would provide best growing conditions?

Other Language Ideas

Have you ever found anything interesting buried in the earth? What did you find and how? What else could be buried in the earth? What is an archaeologist? What would you like to find if you were an archaeologist?

Earth

Mix some mud-coloured paint and make shoe prints with old shoes

Can you match the shoes to the prints?

Visit local museum to look at local finds. If possible, organise small excavation in school grounds.

Class story about an old key or box dug up from newly ploughed earth. What happens? Make large class book, with groups of children working on writing each part of the story.

Expressions — 'salt of the earth', 'earthy', 'earth mother', 'down to earth'.

Other Activities

Start school garden.

Discuss different ways of feeding and improving soil — why is it necessary?

Make own compost heap.

Look at ways of working the soil,
- a) in other cultures. How does climate affect what is grown?
- b) long ago.

Visit museum which has collections of agricultural implements.

Books and Stories

Talkabout Soil, by Angela Webb, Franklin Watts.

In the Soil, by Ralph Whitlock, Wayland.

Meg's Veg, by Jan Piénkowski, Picture Puffin.

Thumbelina, Trad.

Poems and Rhymes

'The Digging Song', by Wes Magee, *A Very First Poetry Book,* OUP.

'Mole', by Alan Brownjohn in *Four Seasons Poetry Books* (Summer), Macdonald & Co. Ltd.

'The Mud', by Andrew Young, *Four Seasons Poetry Books* (Spring), Macdonald & Co. Ltd.

Songs and Music

'The Hippopotamus Song', Flanders and Swann, in *Children's Rainyday Songbook,* Chappell Music Ltd.

'God Speed the Plough', Trad. in *A Musical Calendar of Festivals,* Ward Lock Educational.

'Ground' in *Songs from Play School,* A & C Black.

Pictures to look at

'The Ploughed Field', John Sell Cotman, 1807 (watercolour).

'Large piece of turf', Albrecht Dürer, 1503.

Display Board

Background — bright yellow paper. Build up left-hand side of board with crumpled newspaper and old boxes stapled to board. Cover with old brown fabric, creating dips and hollows as shown. Cut holes in fabric; arrange soft toys — fox, mole etc. — in position.

Grass — either grow real grass seeds in margarine tubs and position in 'hollows' or make grass from stiff paper and dried grasses painted green. Dab fabric with PVA glue and sprinkle on soil/grit. Add other toy animals, worms, snails, beetles. Letters of 'earth', 'soil', 'ground' — brown paper on orange.

Children's drawings of garden tools. Individual pictures backed in dark brown. **Border** — sponge-printed in shades of brown.

Display Table

Brown or yellow fabric. Use PVC fabric under mud-printing area. Pots of seeds growing in different soils. Soil samples. Root vegetables. Vivarium. Children's models of ants. Books of children's writing. Reference books. Bowl of mud, brushes, spoons and paper for making mud prints.

Volcanoes

Discussion and Observation/Science Ideas

What is a volcano? Where do they occur? Look at the areas of volcanic activity on world map and globe. How are volcanoes formed? Investigate famous eruptions long ago and more recently. **Visit** a museum with displays and models of volcanoes. Talk about the formation of the Earth and subsequent cooling to form the Earth's crust. Examine some pumice stones — discuss texture/colour/weight; floating and sinking; how we use pumice. What are geysers, hot springs and mud pools? Volcanoes in mythology — Vulcan; the Hawaiian goddess, Madam Pele.

Art and Craft

Eruption pictures; **background** — royal blue paint covered with PVA. **Volcano** — sponge printed, or rubbings of rock/stone/concrete using Conté crayon, pastel or wax crayons in shades of grey, brown and black on white paper; **or** glue creased paper into volcano shape to the background and paint. **Eruption/lava** — mix paint to thick, creamy consistency in reds, yellows, orange metallic colours (gold) and fluorescent colours. Splatter with different brushes or blow with straws to represent lava being thrown up into the air. When dry, lightly smudge crushed charcoal and white chalk where required to represent smoke and ash. **Lava flowing down volcano** —apply large blobs of paint to run down. Tilt paper to allow paint to change direction slightly.

Mosaic pictures — look at Roman mosaics for inspiration and make own using small squares of coloured foils and papers, or eggshell mosaics on card, coated with PVA.

Maths

3D shapes. Collect and make other cone/pyramid shaped objects.
Time — frequency of eruptions.

Musical Activities

Make rhythm patterns using the name of volcanoes:—

Krakatoa   Mount Etna   Surtsey   Vesuvius

Cooking

Volcano food — Krakatoa bangers: Make cone from hot, cooked, mashed potatoes. Stud with sausages. Dribble ketchup from top of 'volcano'.

Books and Stories

Volcano by Lionel Bender in 'The Story of the Earth', Wayland.
Let's Look at Volcanoes by Graham Rickard, Wayland.

Poems and Rhymes

'Mount Etna, A Volcano in Sicily', by Virgil, trans. by C. D. Lewis in *The Kingfisher Book of Children's Poetry*, Guild Publishing.

Display Board

Background — paper behind volcano — deep blue. Bright orange paper at sides. Mount pictures with black and white. Letters of 'volcanoes' cut from gold foil using pinking shears, on black or white pinked paper.
Vocabulary — black writing on white, backed with bright colours.

Display Table

Blue or orange fabric to match board. **Volcano** — plywood or hardboard base. Firmly glue egg boxes or other junk boxes into rough pyramid shape. Cover with chicken wire or wire mesh. Paste on layers of newspaper strips. Form crater at the top. Allow to dry well. Coat with final layer of plaster of Paris. When dry, paint and coat with PVA and sprinkle with gravel here and there. Arrange a few small rocks at the bottom. **Lava** — thick paint mixed with PVA, fluorescent papers, Cellophane, foils, glitter, red and gold lametta, strings of sequins. Glue into crater to give effect of lava bubbling and flowing down volcano. **Smoke** as before.

Also on table — children's own decorated cone/pyramid shapes. Made figure or doll, dressed as Vulcan. Book of children's writing. Factual books about volcanoes and the formation of the Earth; pumice stones, world map showing the 'volcano belt'. Cut long strips of gold foil into flowing lava shapes, and staple to front of table.

Earthworms

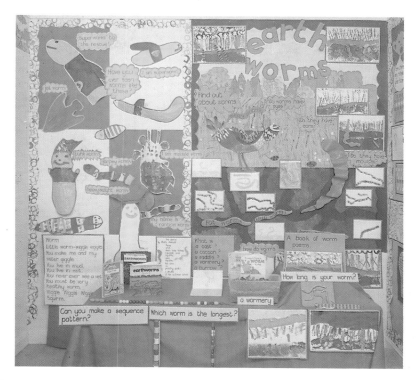

Discussion and Observation/Science Ideas

Go on a worm hunt. Where and when is it easiest to find worms? Look at worms carefully. Do they have eyes/ears/mouths? Can you tell which is the head end and which is the tail? How do worms move? Do they have legs? Look at different kinds of worms. What are the differences? Why are worms good for the soil? What are worm casts? Talk about meaning of male and female — point out worms are both male and female. Where is the saddle and what is its function? What animals eat worms?

Other Science Ideas

Make a wormery.
Put a worm on to a sheet of paper. Listen carefully. What happens when you put a worm on a smooth, shiny surface?

Art and Craft

Line drawings from observation — use coloured pencils, thin crayons, pencils on white paper.
Finger printed worms — use thick brown paint on white paper.
Worm pictures: **Earth** — print with sponge and toilet roll in shades of brown. **Grass** — print with edge of card in shades of green. **Sky** — print with sponge or toilet roll in shades of blue. Cut out worms from brown paper and glue to picture. Add cut out leaf prints.
'Fun' worms — use lots of brightly coloured and fluorescent paint plus collage materials.

Maths

Count number of worms found in a given area.
Make worms by threading beads either for sequence patterns or for counting.

Other Language Ideas

Vocabulary — wormery, worm cast, burrow, cocoon, saddle, mate, male, female.
Read 'Earthworm' by Leonard Clark in *Rhyme Time*. Write own worm-shaped poem.

Books and Stories

Earthworms by Terry Jennings in 'Into Science' Series, OUP.
It's Easy to Have a Worm to Stay by Caroline O'Hagan, Chatto & Windus.
The Worm Book by Janet and Allan Ahlberg in 'Read Together' Series, Piccolo.

Poems and Rhymes

'Earthworm' by Leonard Clark in *Rhyme Time* by Barbara Ireson, Beaver Books.
'Worm' by Karla Kuskin in *Rhyme Time 2,* Beaver Books.

Songs and Music

'Wiggly Woo' in *Sing a Song One,* Thomas Nelson.
'Lots of Worms' in *Birds and Beasts,* A & C Black.

Display Board

(In two sections)
Section 1 — letters of 'earthworms' — orange on green. **Soil** — sponge-printed in brown. **Grass** — printed with card edge in shades of green on green paper. **Sky** — yellow sponge-printed evening sky. Red crêpe border. **Large bird** — use paint and collage materials. **Large worm** — painted brown and coated with PVA. Section 2 — pink and white chequerboard. Printed border.

Display Table

Orange fabric. Wormery, Plasticine worms, bead worms.

Snakes

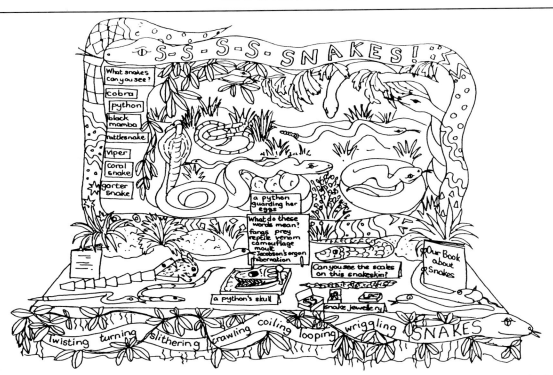

Discussion and Observation/Science Ideas

What kind of animal is a snake? Compare with other vertebrate animals. What do they look/feel like? How do they reproduce, move and feed? Look at the ways snakes catch and kill prey. Using both maps and globe find areas where snakes are most common. Look at sizes, patterns and markings. Why do snakes shed their skins? Which animals catch and kill snakes? **Visit** reptile house at zoo.

Art and Craft

Draw snake from observation or from picture. Carefully observe and record colour markings and pattern of scales. Discuss camouflage.

Make own snakes from junk.

Paint a snake in the middle of a large sheet of paper. Paint outline in bright colour, repeating this process in different colours until paper is full. How does the shape change?

Maths

Make your own snakes and ladders game.

Make snake collection — toy snakes, draught excluders, fur fabric and rubber snakes. Measure in centimetres. Arrange in order of size.

Other Language Ideas

Cut snake-shaped white paper — write snake words — hisss, sssnake, ssslither

Can you think of any more?

Books and Stories

Poisonous Snakes by Colin McCarthy, Franklin Watts.

Snakes by David Lambert, Franklin Watts.

'Rikki-Tikki-Tavi' by Rudyard Kipling in *Stories for Eight Year Olds,* ed. Sara and Stephen Corrin, Puffin.

Poems and Rhymes

'Are You Sitting Comfortably?' by Ian Serraillier in *Another Second Poetry Book,* OUP.

'Snake Glides' by Keith Bosley in *Poems for Nine Year Olds and Under,* Kit Wright, Puffin.

Songs and Music

'Nyangara the Python' (Zimbabwe) retold by Hugh Tracey in *The Singing Sack,* A & C Black,.

'Viper' in *Silly Aunt Sally* by Jan Holdstock, Ward Lock Educational.

Picture to look at

'The Snake', David Hockney.

Display Board

Large snake picture: **sky** — clear or bright blue paper. **Ground** — golden sand — paint with bright yellow paint and allow to dry. Coat with PVA and sprinkle with glitter and sand. **Trees** — paint tree trunks with thick, brown paint and comb into bark patterns or sponge print in shades of brown. **Leaves** — cut from variety of fabrics and paper in shades of green. **Plants** — cut leaves/fronds from green paper, foil, lametta. Staple to background. **Snake border** — make in sections. Either leave plain colour or decorate sections using collage materials, crayon, paint and oil pastel. Work with shades of one or two colours only. Writing — on white paper backed with black.

Display Table

Fabric colour to match 'sand'. Arrange rocks where required. Sprinkle table with sand. Foliage — use real pot plants or make leaves from papers; tie bunch together and place in small pots behind rocks. Others items as shown. Children's writing; books and stories.

Front of table — writing on white or orange snake. Make creepers from string or frayed ropes. Paint green/brown; attach cut-out paper and fabric leaves, green lametta. Staple or pin carefully to front, looping creepers around snake.

Bats

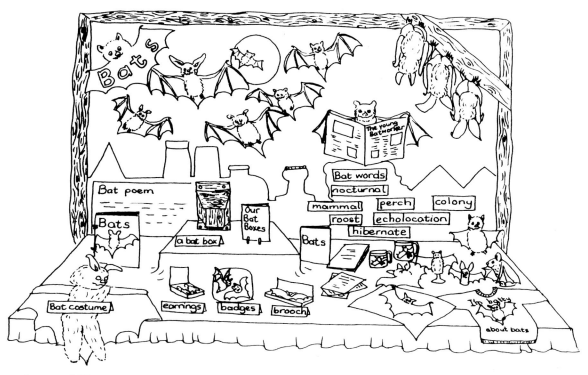

Discussion and Observation/Science Ideas

What sort of animal is a bat? Why are some people afraid of them? Discuss myths about bats — what are the facts? What do bats look like? How do they eat/sleep and where do they live? **Visit** zoo or natural history museum to observe and make drawings. Some species of bat are less common now than they used to be — why? Find out what is being done to protect bats. Invite member of local Bat Protection Group to talk to the children and investigate the possibility of putting up a bat box. Find out about different species of bats. How do bats find their way about? What is echo-location? Talk about echoes — how can we make our voices echo? Can we find our way about using sound instead of sight? (Blindfold a willing child — ask another child to stand still and make sounds. Can blindfolded child locate the sounds?)

Art and Craft

Make 2D or 3D bats out of waste packaging and fabric scraps — bodies of toilet rolls or yoghurt pots; limbs from spent matchsticks, iced lolly sticks, twigs; wings from black binliners or card. Cover body and make head from furry fabric; ears — felt or card. Fasten limbs with glue, paper fasteners or staples. Can you find ways to make the wings move?

Bat pictures — night sky, painted royal blue or purple; silver foil and glitter moon; collage bats — fur fabric, felt, binliners. Cut wing shapes from black card and attach to bat body in such a way that wings stand out from paper.

Make a bat mobile.

Make bat finger puppets.

Maths

Talk about 'spans'. Draw bats with different wing spans. Area of wings using squared paper.

Other Language Ideas

Vocabulary — colony, sonar, nocturnal, membrane, roost, echo-location.

Factual writing about bats.

Books and Stories

Bats, 'Life Cycle' Books by Althea, Longman.
Discovering Bats, Jane Mulleneux, Wayland.
Chocolate Mouse and Sugar Pig by Irina Hale, Picture Macs.

Poems and Rhymes

'Bat Chant', Liz Lochhead, *Kingfisher Book of Comic Verse,* selected by Roger McGough, Kingfisher Books.
'Batty', Shel Silverstein, *Kingfisher Book of Comic Verse.*
'The Bat', Ogden Nash in *Custard and Company,* selected by Quentin Blake, Puffin.

Songs and Music

'Boris the Bat' in *Ralph McTell's Alphabet Zoo Songbook,* Ward Lock Educational.

Display Board

Sky — royal blue or purple. White moon sprinkled with glitter or sequins. **Border** — brown paper painted in darker brown or black to achieve wood-grain effect. **Crossbeam** made from cardboard (glue small boxes along reverse side — staple to board as shown for 3D effect). Hang toy or model bats from beam. Children's bats flying in sky; black silhouettes of buildings.

Display Table

Fabric to match sky — children's models of bats, toy bats, bat brooches, mugs, badges, bat box. Use fabric paints or pens to design bat tea-towels, sweatshirts and T-shirts. Make bat costume with fur fabric and binliners.

The Pied Piper

Discussion and Observation/Science Ideas

Read poem and one or two of the story versions. Discuss the story. Why did the people of Hamelin wish to rid the town of rats? What damage did the rats do? What did the Pied Piper say to the Mayor? How much money was he promised?

Discuss the role of rats in spread of disease, including plague. Are there rats today? Where? What do they look like? How do they feed? Describe methods of rat control today and during the last century.

Does anyone have a pet rat or mouse? Care of pet rats and mice. Try to obtain a live white rat/mouse as class pet. Observe carefully and keep class log book, recording food preferred, grooming habits, rate of growth if animal is very young, movements, sleeping habits. In what ways do rats differ from mice?

Find Hamelin on map. Find pictures of medieval and old towns, and look at everyday life for ordinary people in the Middle Ages.

Look at different wind instruments. Which was most likely to have been the Pied Piper's pipe? Listen to recorded examples.

Art and Craft

Careful drawings of rats from observation. Use charcoal, Conté crayons, pastels, oil pastels, pencils, on white cartridge paper. Explore ways of creating fur-like texture and sharp claws/teeth.

Draw or paint Hamelin with its wood-framed medieval houses. Include the River Weser and the Town Hall.

Design posters warning of the plague of rats, or advising on methods of control.

Design costume for Pied Piper — sketch ideas first, then assemble as collage using variety of fabrics, ribbons, feathers, sequins, braids, beads.

Colour sorting — find as many different reds or yellows as you can using collage materials.

Models of rats from papier mâché, clay, or junk boxes — paint finished rat or glue on fur fabric to cover rat's body.

Maths

Make rat/Pied Piper 'shape pictures' — use ready-cut or plastic shapes to draw around.

Make own rat game — e.g. similar to 'Flounders' — or play 'Three Blind Mice' or 'Mousie Mousie'.

Using children's rat models, group into sets by size, colour and construction.

Ordering of sizes — measure model rats in cms., weigh in grams.

Money — compare currencies in different countries. Which country uses guilders today? What is used in modern Germany? Were the guilders in coins or notes? Make 1,000 guilders in notes. Design 1 guilder, 5, 10 and 100 guilder notes. Use for counting in 5's, 10's, 100's. Explore ways of mass-producing the guilders, or collect bottle-tops or foil from chocolate coins.

The Pied Piper

A thousand guilders! Come, take fifty!

Folks who put me in a passion May find me pipe to another fashion!

How did the Pied Piper feel? Why? Draw a picture.

Other Language Ideas

Where did the Pied Piper take the children? Describe your ideal place to live.

Write a letter from one of Hamelin's inhabitants to someone in another town, describing the rat problem.

Rat words — scampering, scrabbling, pouncing, whisking, scuttling, omniverous, rodent, gnawing.

Discussion — how would you get rid of a plague of rats?

Rat/mouse expressions — 'to smell a rat', 'you dirty rat', 'you ratted on me', 'quiet as a mouse', 'are you a man or mouse?'

Look at other poems which tell a story.

Describe the Pied Piper.

Music Activities

Set story of Pied Piper to music, making up short pieces to illustrate different aspects of the story. Use tuned and untuned percussion.

Listen to simple medieval tunes and then make up own on chime bars or recorder. Accompany with tambour, tambourine or bells.

Movement/Drama

Mime scenes from the story, using facial expressions and body movements to convey anger, fear, joy and horror where appropriate.

Books and Stories

Taking Care of your Mice and Rats, by Joyce Pope, Franklin Watts.

The Pied Piper, illustrated by Catherine Storr, Methuen.

The Pied Piper, by Val Biro, OUP.

Poems and Rhymes

'The Rat', Andrew Young, in *Of Caterpillars, Cats and Cattle*, Puffin.

'He Was a Rat,' anon. in *Poems for 9 Year Olds and Under*, Puffin.

'Sid the Rat', Eleanor Oliphant, as above.

Songs and Music

'Tom he was a Piper's Son', Trad.

Picture to look at

'Rat Catchers', Sir Edwin Landseer, 1821.

Display Board

Border of red and yellow triangles. Letters of 'The Pied Piper of Hamelin' in red backed with black on gold foil 'scroll'.

Picture of scene from story. **Sky** — rag-rolled in shades of blue. **Houses** — individually painted in cream/dark brown. **Roofs** — either print tiles with small circular lids or cut tiles from variety of suitable papers. Glue on in overlapping fashion. **Cobblestones** — print in shades of grey/brown. Attach long boxes — such as Clingfilm boxes — to table where it meets the board, to form edge of 'road'. Cover with 'cobbles'. **Money bag** — cut from hessian; gold chocolate coins/bottle tops for guilders. **Individual characters** — paint, paper/fabric collage. Writing on white paper, backed in red.

Display Table

River — shiny blue or turquoise fabric. Add silver lametta or strips of foil. Children's rat models, different versions of the story, other rat stories and books, instruments.

Foxes

Discussion and Observation/Science Ideas

Use selection of fox stories as starting points. What is the fox like in these stories? Who has seen a real fox? What do they look like? Look at size, how and where they live, their food and feeding habits, in which countries they are found. Why have fox numbers in urban and suburban areas increased in recent years? **Visit** a natural history museum or local wildlife sanctuary for injured animals. Look at shape of fox. Which other animal does a fox resemble? Why? Foxhunting — arguments for and against.

Art and Craft

Drawing from observation at visit to sanctuary or museum: use crayons, pencil, oil pastels.
Scraperboard pictures — use wax crayons, thickly and evenly applied. Explore ways of achieving fur texture using different tools for scraping.
Fabrics — sort to find appropriate colours and textures. Use in collages.
Paper collage/mixed media — use variety of techniques to achieve fur texture — fringing, glueing down one end only of torn/cut strips; printing with card edges and brushing paint with stiff toothbrush.

Maths

Time — differences between night and day. What does 'nocturnal' mean? Which animals are mainly nocturnal? Compare length of time from birth to independence in foxes and humans.

Other Language Ideas

Read the poem 'Four Little Foxes'. What is happening in the poem, and why? Tell or write the story.
Traps and snares — why were they used and by whom?
Vocabulary — vixen, dog fox, earth, brush, cubs, mammal.

Books and Stories

Discovering Foxes, by Miranda MacQuilty, Wayland.
Foxy Fables, Tony Ross, Picture Puffins.

Poems and Rhymes

'Four Little Foxes', by Lew Sarett in *The Golden Treasury of Poetry*, selected by Louis Untermeyer, Collins.
'A Fellow Mortal', by John Masefield in *Of Caterpillars, Cats and Cattle*, Puffin.

Songs

'Old Daddy Fox' in *The Funny Family*, Ward Lock Educational.
'A Hunting we will go', *Clarendon Book of Singing Games, Book 1*, OUP.

Picture to look at

'The Last Run of the Season', Sir Edwin Landseer, 1851.

Display Board

Large picture of café scene from 'The Fox and the Stork' in *Foxy Fables*. **Background**— bright yellow paper. **Foxes/storks** — collage of fabric and paper. 3D limbs, beaks, noses, tongues. **Large fox in centre** — paint fox head, coat with PVA. Letters of 'Foxes' — fluorescent orange paper. Paint body. Writing on white paper, backed with fluorescent orange. Staple to fox. Children's individual pictures backed in black and orange.

Display Table

Fabric to match board. Real dishes/sundae glasses — or make with waste materials and packaging. Make cone from clear plastic, push narrow end into decorated yoghurt pot or similar. Discuss stability of design. Fill with ice-cream sundae — cotton wool balls, red beads, with chocolate sauce of brown paint mixed with PVA. Fox poems on cards, pie charts, books of children's writing, books and stories, children's models and toy foxes.

Trees

Discussion and Observation/Science Ideas

Go out and look at different trees. What is a tree? How does it grow? Look at shape, colour, size, texture of leaves. Note differences.What do leaves do? Look at trees at different times of the year. Why do some trees lose their leaves? Why do trees have fruit/seeds/nuts/berries? How are these dispersed? Look at winged fruits. Which fruits are poisonous? Discuss the value of trees to humans and to our environment. What is happening to the tropical rain forests? What are the repercussions? What are the effects of acid rain on trees? Discuss the work of Forestry Commission.

Other Science Ideas

Use your five senses: look at trees; touch and feel bark and leaves; hear/listen to rustling of leaves; taste edible fruits; smell — what can you smell?

Make a log environment in a quiet corner outside. Observe wildlife that colonise it. Keep 'log book'.

Art and Craft

Look at artists' pictures of trees. Make individual drawings/paintings of trees in different seasons: **Spring** — background — sponge print sky in shades of blue; sponge print grass in shades of green, including fluorescent; overprint with card edge for grassy effect. (Try mixing fluorescent yellow paint with green powder colour.) Blossom — print with flat end of pencil or fingertip.

Summer — Sponge print leaves in shades of green.

Autumn — Print leaves in shades of brown, orange, yellow, crimson. Could add 'leaves' cut out of gold/red foil.

Winter — background — either snow scene or sunset using paints or pastels. Bare trees painted or crayonned in shades of brown or black, or blow thin paint through a straw into tree shape.

Maths

Collect conkers, pine cones and acorns and use for weighing/balancing activities.

Look at trees in immediate area. Draw a map locating trees. Make a census chart.

Other Language Ideas

Vocabulary — tree names, branch, root, twig, bud, sapling, evergreen, deciduous, coniferous, simple and compound leaves.

Trees in mythology/history/Bible — superstitions and beliefs.

Books and Stories

Trees by David Burnie, 'Eye Witness Guides', (in association with the Natural History Museum), DK Ltd.
The Willow Maiden by Meghan Collins, Methuen.

Poems and Rhymes

'Trees' by S. Coleridge in *The Book of a Thousand Poems*, Bell & Hyman.
'Trees' by Walter de la Mare as above.

Songs and Music

'Lazy Coconut Tree' in *Trig Trog*, OUP.

Pictures to Look At

'Fruit Trees in Blossom', Van Gogh , (Spring).
'Path Through the Woods', Pissarro, (Summer).

Display Board

Background — divide board into four and back with seasonal colours. Letters of 'trees' — green on yellow.

Display Table

Covered in green and yellow fabric. Logs, leaves, cones, conkers, acorns etc.

Potatoes

Discussion and Observation/Science Ideas

Visit a greengrocer's or supermarket to look at and buy a variety of potatoes. Which method of cooking suits which variety? Where and how do potatoes grow? What sort of vegetable is a potato? Look carefully at outside of potato. What does it feel/smell like? Peel potato and leave overnight. What happens? How do you like your potatoes cooked? Compare tastes and smells of fried, boiled, baked, roast and chipped potatoes. Make favourite potato recipe. Collect a variety of potato products. Which do you like best? Nutritional value of potatoes. History of potatoes — where did they originate? Look at world map. Were they always eaten by humans? When were potatoes introduced into Britain, and by whom?

Art and Craft

Potato printing.

Drawing from observation using permanent felt-tip pens or black crayon. Add colour with thin water colour, pastels, or oil pastels.

Pictures of growing potato plant — use gummed paper, tissue and crayon on white paper.

Make potato 'people' — use cocktail sticks, lolly sticks, pieces of other vegetables, twigs, acorns or use junk materials.

Maths

Weighing and balancing activities.
Price of potatoes.

Other Language Ideas

Read 'The Clever Potato' by Vernon Scannell. Re-tell in own words.

Books and Stories

Potatoes by Dorothy Turner, Wayland.
The Potato by Raphaêlle Brice, Pocketworld, Moonlight Publishing Ltd.

Poems and Rhymes

'The Clever Potato' and 'Versatile Murphy' by Vernon Scannell, both from *The Clever Potato*, Beaver Books.

Songs and Music

'One potato, two potato', *Appuskidu*, A & C Black.
'Ten potatoes/This old man', from *Silly Aunt Sally*, Ward Lock Educational.

Pictures to look at

'Bowl with potatoes', Van Gogh, 1888.
'Still-life with basket of potatoes', Van Gogh, 1885.

Display Board

Background — centre panel: pale blue sky, brown sponge printed earth. **Potato plant** — paint and paper collage. **Remainder of board** — green/white chequerboard. **Border** — orange crêpe. Letters of 'potatoes' — brown on orange.

Display Table

Covered in orange fabric. Varieties of potatoes, potato products, scales and weights.

Oranges and Lemons

Discussion and Observation/Science Ideas

Look at different kinds of oranges and lemons. What do they feel/smell like? Look at structure and pattern. Cut up and taste. Which taste do you like best? Where do oranges and lemons come from? Find countries on map of the world. Which products contain oranges/lemons? Collect different orange and lemon drinks. Compare tastes. Find out which has highest fruit content. Look at labels and compare ingredients. Which drink is healthiest? Which do you like best? Which products contain orange/lemon fragrance?

Science Activities

Plant pips — label and monitor growth.
Squeeze fruit — how do we get the juice out? Could make jelly.

Art and Craft

Print with cut up oranges and lemons. Use different shades of bright fluorescent orange and lemon paint.
Line drawings from observation of half an orange/lemon. Use pencils, oil pastels, felt-tip pens, pencil crayons.
Design labels for marmalade/drinks.
Paper collage of oranges and lemons — slices, segments, whole fruit. Use variety of papers — gummed, Cellophane, tissue, wrapping papers.

Maths

Peel orange and count segments.
Investigate halves, quarters.
Shape pictures — cut out circle of gummed/fluorescent paper, fold and cut out sectors. Fit back into circle or into a pattern.

Other Language Ideas

Vocabulary — citrus, rind, pith, peel, juice, pip, segment, sector, zest, slice, sour, sweet, bitter.
Describe the appearance/taste of an orange/lemon.

Books and Stories

Citrus fruit, by Susan Wake, Wayland.
An Orange for the baby by Tessa Potter, Readalong Stories, OUP.

Poems and Rhymes

'The King's Breakfast', A.A. Milne, *A Packet of Poems,* OUP.
'Oranges', Dave Calder, *Another Fourth Poetry Book,* OUP.

Songs and Music

'Oranges and lemons', in *A Musical Calendar of Festivals*, Ward Lock Educational.
'Just a squeeze of lemon', Mary Martin and Valerie Stumbles, in *Sing a Song of Celebration*, Cassell.

Picture to look at

'Tropiques', Henri Rousseau, 1907.

Display Board

Background — orange and lemon chequerboard, orange border. Letters of 'oranges and lemons' — orange and lemon paper on black. **Large orange and lemon tree** — sponge printed in shades of green; leafy shapes painted on at random. **Oranges and lemons** — some cut out of fluorescent paper, some painted, as shown.

Display Table

Orange and lemon fabric. Orange/lemon drinks, products containing orange/lemon flavours or fragrances; basket of oranges and lemons; globe, atlas; pots containing planted orange and lemon pips; half an orange and lemon.

Glass

Discussion and Observation/Science Ideas

Make a collection of glass objects to look at. Discuss colour, feel, weight, reflections, shapes. Is it rough or smooth, warm or cool, transparent or translucent? Uses of glass — different types needed for windows in buildings, cars, cookware, spectacles. Decorative glass — ornaments, stained glass windows, jewellery. Arrange **visit** to see glass blower at work. Mirrors — look at concave and convex mirrors. Experiment with reflections. Lenses and their uses. What happens when glass breaks? Compare breaking of ordinary glass to shatterproof glass. Why and where is shatterproof glass used? How is glass made? What materials are used? Recycling glass — what are bottle banks? Who has seen one? How and why is glass re-cycled? Glass long ago — how was it made and what were its uses? **Visit** museum to see examples of old glass. Common sense safety precautions with glass.

Art and Craft

Visit a church which has stained glass windows. Draw a stained glass window using bright crayons, oil pastel or felt-tips.

Make stained glass windows — cut shape from black sugar paper. Fold and cut out smaller shapes to form a pattern or design. Glue on coloured tissue or Cellophane.

Draw glass objects from observation — jugs, vases or bottles containing water; dish of marbles, wine glasses. Observe highlighted areas and areas in shade — use smudged charcoal, white chalk, black and white crayons or oil pastels.

Draw what you can see in a mirror.

Design a magic mirror — look at examples of decorated mirror frames.

'Through the window' pictures — draw the window and frame and what can be seen outside. Glue on fabric curtains. Use crayon, felt-tips, oil pastels.

Maths

Magnification with hand lens.

Weighing and balancing with marbles.

Capacity work with glass bottles and containers. Can you empty one bottle into another using a syphon?

Windows of different shapes. Where can you see round or arched windows?

Symmetry using mirrors.

Look at different styles and tessellating patterns of window panes. Make own tessellating pattern.

Sort glass containers into shape, size and colour.

Other Language Ideas

Re-tell the story of 'The Glass Slipper' or 'The Little Old Woman in the Vinegar Bottle', Trad.

Vocabulary — molten, furnace, lehr, crystal, cullet.

Find as many words as you can to describe a glass ornament, vase or glass object seen in museum visit.

Expressions and proverbs — 'glassy-eyed', 'glassy stare', 'glazed look', 'people who live in glass houses shouldn't throw stones'.

Factual writing about glass — production, uses, glass through the ages, decorative and ornamental glass.

Write a message in a bottle.

Glass

Read 'The Old Woman who Lived in a Vinegar Bottle' (trad.)

Would you like to live in a bottle?

Musical Activities
Collect different sized bottles. Find ways of making sounds — blowing and tapping with bottles full, half full or empty. Try to make a scale.

Make a tape recording of different sounds made with glass — milk bottles or wine glasses clinking; rattling marbles; breaking glass; stirring a drink; eating from a glass dish. Children can describe and identify sounds.

Cooking
Compare glass and metal saucepans. Which, if either, is quicker to boil a liquid? Advantages and disadvantages of cooking with glass.

Other Ideas
Make bottle garden (or use large jar).
Set up marble run. Collect variety of marbles for games.

Books and Stories
Glass by Jane Chandler, A & C Black.
The Magic Mirror Book by Marion Walter, Hippo.
A Pocketful of Games with Marbles by Ruth Thomson, Hippo Books, Scholastic Publications.
Weird Windows by Charlotte Firmin, André Deutsch.

Poems and Rhymes
'The Window Cleaner' by M. Long in *The Young Puffin Book of Verse*.
'In the Mirror' by Elizabeth Fleming in *Once Upon a Rhyme*, Puffin.

Songs and Music
'Johnny's Lost His Marble' in *Kokoleoko*, Macmillan Education Ltd.
'The Mirror', Trad. Dutch, in *The Clarendon Book of Singing Games, Book II*, OUP.

Picture to look at
'Still Life on a Glass Table', David Hockney, 1971-72.

Display Board
Background — orange, red or yellow. Border — glue pieces of string, pasta shapes, buttons and lids to strips of thin card. Spray with gold paint. Poems — on white paper backed with black. **Mirror** — real, or use sheet of new foil on black paper. **Window** — paint sky/clouds on large sheet of paper. Cover with clear plastic. Glue on brown/black paper frames. **Window cleaner** — real cloth in hand. **Ladder** — make from cardboard strips. **Stained glass window** — cut window frame from white card. Make pattern with coloured acetate, Cellophane or tissue. Glue to card. Glue on black paper frame. If using tissue, coat with PVA. Letters of 'glass' — same technique as for stained glass window. Cut out letters and back with gold foil. Children's pictures backed in black, white or bright colours.

Display Table
Shiny fabric — colour to match board. Terrace with boxes. Fibre glass curtain, draped as shown. Bottle bank made from old box, painted. Other items, books and lenses, as shown; book of children's writing on jar-shaped paper.

Plastics

Discussion and Observation/Science Ideas

Make a collection of plastic items, including as many different kinds as possible. Discuss their properties. What advantages do man-made fabrics have over natural fabrics? Which type of rainwear is most water resistant? Carry out tests using both fine plant spray and watering can. Record results. Look at a selection of plastic toys. Are they safe? Can they be broken easily? Are there any sharp edges? Talk about the uses of plastics in the kitchen, in household and D.I.Y. products. Disposable plastic — what do we throw away? What happens to it? Bring in plastic packaging. How can we be less wasteful? Can we re-use plastic bottles, polythene and carrier bags, plastic cartons? Some plastics are biodegradable. What does this mean? Can you find any examples? How are plastics made? What is the main raw material and how is it obtained? Study the history of plastics — earliest plastics and their uses. **Visit** museums and look in second-hand shops for examples.

Art and Craft

Plaiting and weaving with strips cut from carrier bags. Plastic collage using plastic scraps of all kinds.

Collage pictures — collect various coloured cleaning and wiping sponges and scourers. Use for background of sky and ground. Add people, trees, animals — with bottletops, plastic buttons, beads.

Make 'stained glass windows' using pieces of coloured cellulose acetate.

Maths

Lay table in home corner with plastic tea set for dolls' tea party.

Other Language Ideas

Look at tray of plastic objects. Remove tray — how many can you remember?

Make people or animals from plastic containers. Write a story about them.

Books and Stories

Plastics by Terry Cash, 'Threads' Series, A & C Black.
Alfie's Feet by Shirley Hughes, Picture Lion.

Poems and Rhymes

'Happiness' by A.A. Milne in *The Christopher Robin Verse Book*, Methuen Children's Books.

Sculpture to look at

Linear Construction No. 2 by Naum Gabo, 1970-71 (Tate Gallery).

Display Board

Background — bright paper given a sheen with PVA. Pictures backed in black or black and white. **Figures** — draw round two children and cut out. Paint flesh colour and coat with PVA. Dress in clothes as shown. Staple to board. **Paddling pool** — make from coloured carrier bags, cut to shape and stapled to board. Add 3D effect by padding with rolled newspaper. Make swimming ring in same way or use old real one. Letters of 'Plastics' cut from different kinds of plastics — foam, polythene, nylon, or cut from fluorescent paper and backed in black. Glue or staple to ring before attaching to board. Poem as shown. Drape lengths of PVC and nylon fabric down one side of board and over terracing on display table.

Display Table

Fabric to match board. Terrace with boxes as shown. Plastic articles as shown. Torn carrier bag attached to figure with 'shopping' spilling on to table. Recycle old plastic bottles to make containers and toys as shown. Children's writing about plastics. Books and stories.

Metals

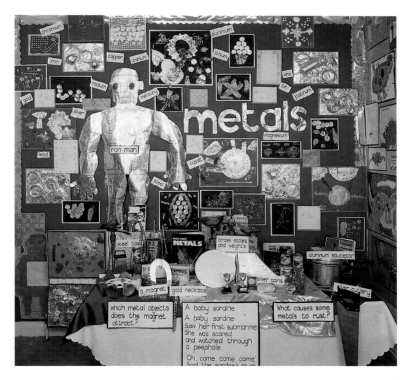

Discussion and Observation/Science Ideas

Make a collection of metal objects. Describe feel, appearance, colour, texture, weight. Reflections — in which metals can you see your reflection? What happens to your reflection when the metal is curved? Where do metals come from and how are they obtained? Look at world production of metals on a map. What is a precious metal? Uses of metal today — **visit** museum to look at earliest uses of metal. Rust — which metals rust? Why does rusting occur? Some metals react with the atmosphere and become dull and tarnished. How can we restore the shine? Magnetism — which metals are attracted to magnets?

Art and Craft

Collect a variety of metal scrap — nails, screws, paper clips, cogs, springs, bottle tops, sequins, tinsel, glitter. Use for collage work.

Brass rubbings at local church.

Look at patterns in metal — wrought iron gates, grilles, fences and architectural details. Observe carefully and draw with very soft pencil, black crayon and felt-tip. Make wrought iron patterns on white paper with string (dyed black) or black wool.

Maths

Weighing and balancing activities with nails, paper clips, screws, bottle tops etc.

Shopping activities with real coins.

Other Language Ideas

Expressions — 'hard as nails/iron', 'nerves of steel', 'good as gold', 'worth his weight in gold'.

Names of metals.

Vocabulary — filigree, silver/gold plating, corrosion, tarnish, alloy, metal ore, shiny, burnished, reflections, smelting seams, blast furnace, foundry, casting.

Musical Activities

Make different sounds using tin cans, lengths of copper tubing suspended from a wooden frame, saucepan lids, bottle tops.

Books and Stories

'The Steadfast Tin Soldier', Hans Anderson, Trad.
Modern Metals by Andrew Langley in 'Science in Action' Series, Wayland.

Poems and Rhymes

'A Baby Sardine' by Spike Milligan in *A Second Poetry Book*, OUP.
'The Kettle' by Gwynneth Thurburn in *Rhyme Time*, Beaver Books.

Songs and Music

'The Blacksmith' in *The Clarendon Book of Singing Games, Book I*, OUP.

Picture/Sculpture to look at

'The Copper Urn', Jean Baptiste Chardin, c. 1734.
'Cyclops' (Bronze sculpture), Sir Eduardo Paolozzi, 1957.

Display Board

Background — dark blue with silver foil border. Letters of 'metals' — silver foil glued on to thin cardboard. Large 'iron man' — silver foil and cardboard.

Display Table

White, blue shiny and silver fabrics. Metal objects, jewellery, magnets etc.

Fabrics

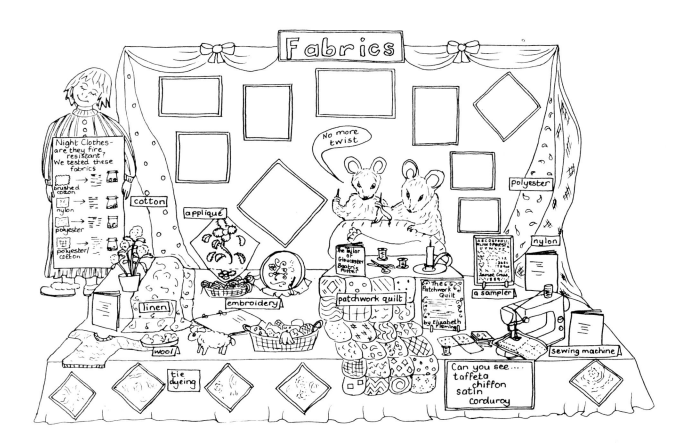

Discussion and Observation/Science Ideas

Make a collection of different fabric samples and clothes. Talk about fabrics which are used to make clothes; natural/man-made fibres. Look at thickness, texture and weight. Which fabrics are used for underwear, warm clothing, summer clothing? Why?

Look at ways in which fabrics are made. Use magnifying glass to examine samples. Is the cloth woven or knitted? Can you see holes between the threads? Can you pull out any of the threads using tweezers? Unravel threads to look at individual fibres.

Set up tests to determine the properties of different fabrics — water resistance, strength, water absorption, resistance to fire, insulation. Record the results. What conclusions can be drawn?

Interpret the symbols on 'care' labels — what do they mean? What happens when clothes are washed in too hot a wash cycle? Which fabrics shrink? Compare effects of hot water on different fabrics.

Look at patterns on cloth; colour, printing and dyeing.

Arrange visits from — lacemaker, hand/machine knitter; people who can demonstrate crochet, embroidery, use of sewing machine.

Visit museums to look at textile crafts and clothes from long ago.

Investigate history of spinning, weaving, cloth-making; clothes around the world for hot and cold climates.

Art and Craft

Weaving with strips of cloth/thick yarn on simple wooden frames.

Simple sewing on binca fabric.

Dyeing and tie-dyeing — colour mixing and patterns.

Fabric painting.

Fabric collage — sort fabric into texture groups first.

Design item of clothing you would like to have for a specific occasion. Look at catalogues for inspiration. What fabric would be suitable? Look at the designs. Which would be practical and comfortable?

Print onto fabric.

Fabrics

Which fabric dries most quickly?

Maths

Sort clothes into groups.

Matching pairs — socks, mittens; tops and bottoms of tracksuits. Which tracksuit is largest/smallest? What sizes are they? Whom do they fit?

Heavy and light — compare weight of clothing fabrics for winter and summer.

Draw outline of each child; 'dress' with fabric, paper or crayon. Label each article of clothing with child's size.

Visit clothing department and investigate different ways of sizing children's clothes. Which is easiest to understand? Are the sizings appropriate for your age group?

Tessellations — patchwork patterns using patterned paper or fabric cut into suitable shapes.

Other Language Ideas

Vocabulary — tight, stretchy, loose, weave, warp, weft, shrink, hem, cuff, collar. Names of fabrics.

'Feeling' games, blindfolded — child is given a piece of fabric and asked to describe it and say where it might be worn/used.

Re-tell story of 'The Emperor's New Clothes'.

Books and Stories

The Patchwork Quilt, by Valerie Flournoy, Picture Puffin.

Apricots at Midnight, by Adèle Geras, Collins.

Fabrics and Yarns, Anne Coleman, Wayland.

'Resources Today' *Textiles*, by Kathryn Whyman, Franklin Watts.

Poems and Rhymes

'Hark, hark, the dogs do bark', Trad.

'The Merchants of London', Trad. in *Sixty Songs for Little Children*, OUP.

'Cotton', by Eleanor Farjeon in *A Puffin Quartet of Poets*.

'The Useful Art of Knitting', by Katherine Craig in *Another Second Poetry Book*, OUP.

Songs and Music

'Reap the Flax', Swedish Folk Song in *A Musical Calendar of Festivals*, Ward Lock Educational.

'The Work o' the Weavers' in *Sing for Your Life*, A & C Black.

'Woolly Hat', in *Penny Whistles*, Contemporary Songs by Mike Moran, Blackie & Son Ltd.

Pictures to look at

'The Weaver', Vincent van Gogh, 1884.

'Mill Worker', L.S. Lowry, 1912.

Display Board

Background — pink or pale blue. Drape lengths of fabric in variety of colours and textures. Individual pictures backed in deeper shade of background colour or black. Letters of 'fabrics' — cut out of brightly coloured felt, decorated with braid, buttons and sequins. Glue letters on to paper the same colour as background and back with black.

Scene from 'The Tailor of Gloucester': **Mice** — fur fabric collage, pink ears. **Coat** — as near as possible to 'cherry-coloured silk'. White doily cuffs, gold doily for braid edging. Samples of appliqué as shown. Cut-out figure in nightshirt as shown, holding chart.

Display Table

Fabric cover to match board, and terraced as shown. Fabric samples, real cotton plant, or make own from wire, brown fabric, tissue and white cotton wool. Sheep's wool. Other items as shown.

Wood

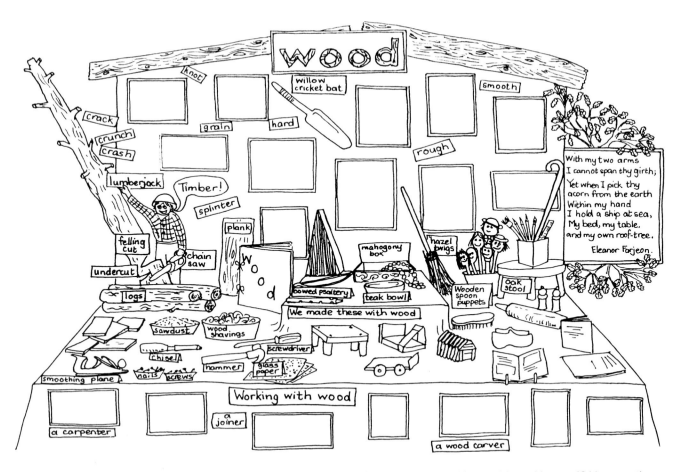

Display board labels: knot, willow cricket bat, smooth, crack, grain, hard, crunch, crash, rough, lumberjack, Timber!, splinter, plank, W o o d, felling cut, chain saw, mahogany box, hazel twigs, undercut, logs, bowed psaltery, teak bowl, Wooden spoon puppets, oak stool, sawdust, wood shavings, We made these with wood, screwdriver, chisel, hammer, glass paper, smoothing plane, nails, screws, Working with wood, a carpenter, a joiner, a wood carver

With my two arms
I cannot span thy girth;
Yet when I pick thy
acorn from the earth
Within my hand
I hold a ship at sea,
My bed, my table,
and my own roof-tree.

Eleanor Farjeon.

Discussion and Observation/Science Ideas

Make collection of wooden things found in classroom, school and home. Try to identify the different woods from which they are made, or sort into similar colours/grain patterns.

Are any special finishes applied to the article (varnish, paint, stain, wax)? How was it assembled? Look for glue, joints, screws. Can you see how many pieces of wood were used?

Look at samples of different woods and compare colour, smell, feel and grain.

Discuss the reasons for the use of wood in building and in furniture making. Look at effects of wet rot, woodworm, weathering. Invite timber preservation expert to talk to the children.

Look at pictures of the trees from which samples came — are they hardwood or softwood? Look at world map and find places where the different kinds of trees are found.

Discuss large scale deforestation in tropical rain forests — why is it harmful? Is there anything we can do?

Talk about the processes involved in obtaining wood — growing, felling, processing at the saw mill, to the finished product. **Visit** — woodyard where children can see wood being cut to shape, and smell and feel the different woods; — a small local furniture workshop where furniture is not mass produced, and where individual stages may be observed.

What tools are used for working with wood? How are they used? What are the safety rules when working with any tools.

Look at samples of chipboard, plywood. How are they made? How is paper made?

Art and Craft

Sculptures/models with wood scraps and offcuts — learn basic skills of sawing with small saw, hammering and using different grades of glasspaper. Use vice if possible for holding wood still. Observe which woods are easiest to work with.

Careful line drawings from observation of knot and grain patterns in different woods or piece of furniture. Use sharpened crayons, fine permanent felt-tip pens in black, then colour wash in thin watercolours in shades of brown; *or* use oil pastels, soft pencils, with darker shades to define grain.

Read *The Little Wooden Horse*. Make individual or class wooden horses, drawing ideas and design on paper first. What is the best way of making and attaching head/ wheels? Provide variety of shapes, sizes and types of wood, including balsa wood, for simple horse shapes.

What is charcoal? Use it to find different ways of making pictures and patterns. Add white chalk to create highlights.

Wood

Make a theatre from an old box.

Teeny Tiny Theatre.

Put on a play with your wooden spoon puppets.

Maths
Measure in cms. while working with wood.
Measure and weigh offcuts of wood — arrange in order of size and weight.
Sort offcuts into hardwood/softwood sets.
Sort wooden toys into sets of those with moving parts and those without.

Other Language Ideas
Vocabulary — lumberjack, felling, chainsaw, timber, log-pond, grading, seasoning, kiln, plywood, chipboard, blockboard, veneer, wood pulp.
Factual writing — make concertina books.
Re-tell your favourite part of the story of *The Little Wooden Horse.*
Make up own stories about a wooden toy.

Musical Activities
Explore different sounds using wooden percussion instruments.
Make own claves or rasps — experiment with different kinds of wood. Make rasps by cutting notches along length of wood or dowelling and then sanding smooth.

Books and Stories
Pinnochio — Trad.
The Little Wooden Horse by Ursula Moray Williams, Puffin.
The Wooden Horse, Great Tales from Long Ago retold by Catherine Storr, Methuen Children's Books.
Focus on Timber by Andrew Langley, Wayland.
Making Pencils by Ruth Thomson, Franklin Watts.
Wood by Kathryn Whyman, 'Resources Today' Series, Franklin Watts.
Wood and Coal, 'Exploring Energy' Series, Macmillan Education Ltd.
Wood by Terry Jennings, 'Threads' Series, A & C Black.

Poems and Rhymes
'Tell Me, Little Woodworm' by Spike Milligan in *Silly Verse for Kids*, Puffin.
'Said the Table to the Chair' by Edward Lear, *A Book of Bosh*, Puffin.
'To an Oak Dropping Acorns' by Eleanor Farjeon in *Four Seasons Poetry Book — Autumn*, compiled by Jennifer Wilson, Macdonald & Co.
'The Chair' by Theodore Roethke in *The Illustrated Treasury of Poetry for Children*, ed. David Ross, Collins.

Songs and Music
'If You Take a Piece of Wood' by Christopher Rowe in *Over and Over Again* by B. Ireson and C. Rowe, Arrow Books.
'Clog Dance' from La Fille Mal Gardée by Louis Hérold.

Picture to look at
'The Wood Sawyers', Jean François Millet, 1850, Victoria and Albert Museum.

Display Board
Background of orange or yellow paper. **Planks** — cut cardboard into plank shapes — paint brown, defining grain with black or dark brown. Letters of 'Wood' — cut from wood-effect vinyl/stained balsa wood/veneer/wood offcuts glued onto white paper or thin card. Back with dark brown. **Lumberjack** — child drawn — 'dress' with paint or fabric collage. **Felled tree** — cut from paper and paint in shades of brown, or glue on brown crêpe paper, creasing it at intervals to give rough, bark-like effect. Add markings with paint in shades of brown. **Oak Twigs** — use card and paper or real oak twigs. Children's pictures backed with brown, orange, yellow or green as appropriate.

Display Table
Fabric to match board. Wood samples, tools, wooden objects, children's models as shown. Books, stories, book of children's writing.

Threads and String

Discussion and Observation/Science Ideas

Read and discuss the story *No Roses for Harry*. Collect variety of string, threads, wools, embroidery silks, cottons. Sort into different types and uses. Unravel thick string and wools. How many strands are twisted together? Why do some need to be thicker than others? What are the threads made from? Talk about different uses of threads and string. Invite local spinner/weaver/lacemaker to demonstrate craft. Look at spiders' webs. Tie shoelaces, ribbons, sashes. Look at different knots and bows. Invite Brown Owl or Akela to demonstrate knots. Problem solving — find the best ways of tying up awkward-shaped or bulky objects and forming a string handle for carrying.

Art and Craft

String painting — fold paper, dip string in paint, place inside folded paper and pull through.

Cut balls of coloured wool, threads and string into pieces. Use in collages.

Weave on simple card looms using wools and string.

Draw spiders' webs. Use silver or gold felt-tips, crayons or white oil pastel on black paper. Add touches of silver glitter or sequins for dewdrops.

Line drawings of string vests and shopping bags, fishermen's nets, knitted dishcloths.

Maths

Use string to measure length, perimeter or circumference of objects.

Tying parcels — estimate amount of string needed.

Other Language Ideas

Vocabulary — weaving, warp, weft, loom, shuttle, ply, purl, plain, rib, cast on, cast off. Names of knots.

Make concertina book — stages in garment production — from sheep to jumper, cotton plant to dress, silkworm to scarf.

Books and Stories

No Roses For Harry by Gene Zion, Picture Puffin.
'The Fable of the Lion and the Mouse', Aesop's fables.
'Rumpelstiltskin', Trad.

Poems and Rhymes

'Henry King' by Hilaire Belloc in *The Puffin Book of Funny Verse* compiled by Julia Watson.
'I Want A Small Piece of String' by Remy Charlip in *The Kingfisher Book of Children's Poetry*, Guild Pub.

Songs and Music

'String a Ring' in *The Clarendon Book of Singing Games, Book II*, OUP.
The Knotted Song in *New Game Songs with Prof. Dogg's Troupe*, BBC Books.

Picture to look at

'The Lacemaker', Jan Vermeer c.1670.

Display Board

Background — bright orange paper. Attach rope ladder to side of board. Children's individual pictures backed in black with red or yellow. Letters of 'threads and string' — use variety of chunky wools and thick string to form letters. Glue on to white paper and back with black. **Harry** — painted on card. **Sweater** — cut old green sweater to fit Harry's body. Unravel long thread and glue sweater in place. Glue on some orange fabric 'roses'. Staple Harry's head and body to board so that feet rest on table. Attach thread to top corner. **Bird** — paper collage. Writing — black on white.

Display Table

Orange fabric cover, terraced with boxes. Parcels, balls of string, articles made from string, ropes of different thicknesses, scissors, knitting. Drape a woven rug, lengths of lace and netting as shown. Hand loom, spinning wheel, basket of straw, reels of gold thread.

Jam

Discussion and Observation/Science Ideas

Who likes jam? What is it? Describe taste and texture. What is it made from?

Bring in a selection of jams — taste and talk about different flavours and colours. Look at labels. Compare proportion of sugar to fruit. What other ingredients are there? Which jam tastes the sweetest? Look at relevant fruit and compare tastes of fruit and jam.

Have a jam picnic.

Visit a 'pick your own' fruit farm, jam making factory or greengrocer.

Science Activities

Make jam. What equipment is needed?

Dissolve sugar in water — compare results in hot and cold water. Find things that dissolve in water and things that don't.

Make jam tarts, buns, sandwiches etc.

Art and Craft

As it is almost impossible to print successfully with soft fruit, alternative suitable shapes could be found — heart-shaped biscuit cutter (strawberry), oval plastic lids (plums), Duplo and Lego bricks (berry fruits).

Experiment with different rubbings on textured surfaces, using crayons in different shades of red, orange and purple. Cut out fruit shapes and make into collage on jam coloured paper.

Collage of fruit shapes — fabrics, coloured papers, gummed papers, magazine cut outs.

Cut out 'jam pot'-shaped white paper. Either print 'fruit' prints or sponge print with jam-coloured paint. Coat with PVA.

Look at different jam labels. Design own labels.

Line drawings of fruit from observation — use thin crayons, oil pastels or soft blendable coloured pencils.

Maths

Capacity — compare jam jars of differing size and shape. How much liquid does each hold?

Weighing — sugar and fruit.

Other Language Ideas

Illustrated sequence story — from fruit to jam pot.

Expressions — 'in a jam', 'traffic jam', 'it's jammed'.

Books and Stories

The Giant Jam Sandwich by John Vernon Lord, Pan.

Jam by Margaret Mahy, Magnet.

Poems and Rhymes

'Bramble Jam' by Irene F. Pawsey in *The Book of a Thousand Poems,* Bell & Hyman.

'Jam' by David McCord in *A Packet of Poems,* OUP.

Songs and Music

'I Can See Cherries' in *Harlequin,* A & C Black.

Picture to look at

'Plums' by William Henry Hunt.

Display Board

Background — fruit printed — strawberry, plum shapes cut out of sponge and printed on to white paper. Red crêpe paper border. Letters of 'jam' — red on fluorescent yellow paper. Children's individual pictures backed in black and red.

Display Table

Red fabric/white strawberry-printed fabric or similar. Variety of jams and soft fruits, real or imitation. Preserving sugar, jam tarts, sponge cakes, doughnuts etc. — either use real or make out of foam or dough. Books and stories. Preserving pan if available.

Bridges

Discussion and Observation/Science Ideas

Who has been on a bridge? Show pictures of famous bridges. **Visit** local or well known bridges. What are bridges for? Discuss construction and type. What are bridges made from? Why? Compare modern bridges with those built long ago.

Maths/Science Activities

Vocabulary — long/longer/longest; high/low; arch; stable/unstable; under/over; narrow/wide.

Make sets of things that go under/over bridges.

Construct own simple bridges of different lengths. How long can you make your bridge before it needs extra support? Do supports need to be evenly spaced? What weight will each bridge support before collapsing? Make bridges from different materials — paper, card, wood, Lego, plastic. Which is the strongest?

Art and Craft

Look again at pictures of famous bridges. Which do you like best and why? Look at decorative features on bridges — line drawings from observation. Look at pattern and texture of bridges. Explore ways of reproducing the effects using printing and collage techniques.

Stand on a bridge and describe what you observe. Make a picture of view from the bridge beginning with the background. Use different techniques to create texture, shape and pattern.

Look at one of the paintings of bridges by Sisley, Monet or other artists. Can you copy the picture?

Other Language Ideas

Talk about the story of Molly Whuppie. Why didn't the Bridge of the One Hair break?

Find places with 'bridge' in the name. Why were they so called?

Drama/PE

Group work — make body bridges, or use planks and benches in apparatus work. Find different ways of crossing the bridges.

Books and Stories

Molly Whuppie by Walter de la Mare, Picture Puffin.
The Bridge Across by Max Bolliger, translated by Anthea Bell, Andersen Press/ Hutchinson.
Bridges by Graham Rickard, Wayland Publications.

Poems and Rhymes

'The Bridge' Leila Berg in *Time for One More,* Magnet, Methuen Children's Books.
'Bridges of the Thames' in *Sing a Song One,* Thomas Nelson & Sons.

Songs and Music

'London Bridge' in *Thirty Folk Settings for Children* by Anne Mendoza and Joan Rimmer, Faber Music Ltd.
'The Forth Bridge' in *Penny Whistles,* Contemporary Songs by Mike Moran, Blackie & Sons.

Picture to look at

'Wooden Bridge at Argenteuil', Sisley, 1872.

Display Board

Background — clear yellow paper. Children's individual pictures backed in black. Letters of 'bridges' — fluorescent orange on black.

Display Table

Yellow fabric to match paper on board. **Bridge** — small rectangular table placed upside down on strong box or bricks. Attach string or cord as shown, glue on narrow strips of balsa wood. **River** — any blue or green fabric that drapes well — add a few strips of silver lametta along length of 'river'. Dolls for bridge. Make model crocodile head. Simple bridges from junk materials. Children's model bridges; books, stories, book of children's writing.

Wheels

Discussion and Observation/Science Ideas

Where do we see wheels? What are they for? Why are they round? Which vehicles have wheels? Find other wheels — cogs, mill wheels, pulleys, spinning wheels. Look at different wheels outside. Why are some big, small, wide, narrow? Discuss wheels in history — chariots, carts, coaches etc.

Maths/Science Activities

Make a model out of junk materials or Lego with a set of moving wheels.

Measure diameter, circumference and radius of wheels.

Trundle wheel to measure distances.

Do wheels have to be round? Make different shaped wheels. Do they roll?

Art and Craft

Observe patterns in wheels. Line drawings from observation — white on black or black on white. Use crayons, Conté crayons, charcoal, chalk, felt-tips.

Make collage of wheel shapes, including cog wheels.

Print wheel shapes using round margarine tubs; print spokes with edge of card.

Make pictures of things with wheels.

Other Language Ideas

Write five sentences about a wheel.

Choose your favourite thing with wheels and describe it.

Movement

Cartwheels, wheelbarrow races, ring games.

Books and Stories

The Lighthouse Keeper's Lunch, Rhonda and David Armitage, Picture Puffin.

Wheels, Science Starters, Macdonald.

Big Wheels by Anne Rockwell, Picture Puffin.

Rachel, The Story of a Child in a Wheel Chair by Elizabeth Fanshawe and Michael Charlton, Bodley Head.

Poems and Rhymes

'Downhill' by Sheila Simmons in *Another First Poetry Book,* OUP.

'Engineers' by Jimmy Garthwaite in *Rhyme Time 2,* Barbara Ireson, Beaver Books.

Songs and Music

'Wheels Keep Turning', *Appuskidu,* A & C Black.

'Keep That Wheel a-Turning', *Ta-ra-ra boom de-ay,* A & C Black.

Picture to look at

'Man in a Wheel Chair', Leon Kossoff, 1959.

Display Board

Background — red and white chequerboard. Red border. Letters of 'wheels' — yellow on red. Windmills mounted on small boxes for 3D effect.

Display Table

Covered in red and white fabric. Children's junk models of things with wheels. Lego models or construction models, cog wheels, water wheel, rotary whisk, children's own windmills.

The Great Fire of London

Discussion

Read and tell story of events. How do we know what happened? Why did the fire spread so quickly?

How were houses constructed at that time? Materials, close proximity of buildings — constant fire risk. What were the weather conditions?

Look at map of old London and follow the fire's progress.

How did people try to stop the fire? Did their methods work? Could such a fire happen in a modern city?

Compare fire services then and now; modern fire safety in buildings — fire drill, extinguishers, smoke detectors.

Fire safety at home and school. How can *we* prevent fire breaking out?

Science Activities

Find out which conditions favour fastest spread of fire, with well-controlled experiments outside, on concrete. Make two piles of twigs/straw/paper both about 2' long and 6" deep. One pile should be damp, the other dry. Light both. Which burns faster? Make a 'wind' by fanning flames — what happens? How can fire be extinguished?

Art and Craft/Language Ideas

Look at life in Stuart London: clothes, music, food, sanitation, hygiene, disease, transport, furnishings, homes. Make pictures or models of different aspects of life in Stuart London using variety of media.

Make fire pictures — use oil pastels, crayons, thick paint or collage materials in appropriate 'fiery' colours.

Visit The Monument and the Stuart section of the Museum of London. Make careful line drawings from observation of something that you find particularly interesting.

Make individual pictures of the Great Fire using paint and collage techniques.

Other Language Ideas

Factual writing about the Great Fire.

Create classroom drama about the Great Fire from the point of view of an ordinary family. Include family argument — should they 'sit tight' or flee the fire? Where should they go? What could they do to help?

Musical Activities

Explore ways of making fire-like sounds with every-day objects or with untuned percussion.

Cooking

Look at 17th century food and cooking. Make a 17th century meal or selection of dishes to sample.

Ideas and recipes can be found in:

Food and Cooking in 17th Century Britain: History and Recipes Peter Brears. Pub. Historic Buildings and Monuments Commission for England.

A Pretty Dinner, described by Gillian Goodwin, Gelofer Press.

The Great Fire of London

Glue boxes onto each other as shown

Print cobbles

Paint walls and beams.
Cut shutters.
Position small dolls in windows.

~ piles of rubbish

Make a model of a London street as it might have been before the fire.

Books and Stories
Excerpts from diaries and memoirs of the time, e.g. Pepys, John Evelyn.
The Fire of London, 'Great Disasters' Series by Rupert Matthews, Wayland.
The Stuarts by Anne Steel, 'Living History' Series, Wayland.
The Great Fire of London by Gustav Milne, Historical Publications Ltd.

Songs About London
'Paul's Steeple', Trad. in *A Second Sixty Songs for Little Children.*
'See-Saw Saccaradown', Trad. in *Brown Bread and Butter,* Ward Lock Educational.
'London's Burning' — round, *Oxford Nursery Song Book,* OUP.

Poems and Rhymes
'The Bells of London', Trad. in *The Poolbeg Book of Children's Verse,* ed. Sean McMahon, Poolbeg Press.
'The Thames', M. M. Hutchison in *The Book of a Thousand Poems,* Bell & Hyman.

Pictures to look at
'The Fire of London', Dutch School, the Museum of London.
'London Before the Fire', Thomas Wyck, c. 1663, (Devonshire Collection, Chatsworth).
'Old London Bridge 1630', Claude de Jongh, Kenwood House.

Display Board
Individual houses painted brown with darker brown timbers. **Windows** — squares of orange fluorescent paper — add narrow strips of black paper to form leaded lights. **Roofs** — cut tiles from paper in shades of brown.

Fire — Cut flames from bright red, orange, yellow and fluorescent paper, marbled or printed paper; foil and Cellophane; also use lametta, strings of sequins, glitter.
Smoke — sponge print lightly in shades of grey/white. Letters of 'London's burning!' — fluorescent orange on black.
Writing on sides of boards — tear out small pieces from round edges of large sheets of white paper. Paint paper with creamy wash. While paper is still wet, dab torn edges with dark brown paint to resemble charring. When dry, write with black felt-tip pen.

Display Table
Dark blue shiny fabric. Toy or model boats. Use play people, pipe cleaner people or any suitable tiny doll for figures. Place in boat as shown, with tiny bundles and boxes for belongings. Oars — paint lollipop sticks dark brown. Book of children's writing. Books about the Fire and about 17th century life.

Front of Table
Children's pictures backed in bright colour.

Fire

Discussion and Observation/Science Ideas

Read 'The Sound of Fire' by Mary O'Neill from *Singing in the Sun.* What do you think fire sounds like? Describe the colours you see when a fire burns. How many different kinds of fire have you seen? Fire is dangerous: talk about fire risks at home. Fire drill at school. Why is this important? **Visit** local fire station. Invite local Fire Prevention Officer to speak to children. What would you do if you discovered a fire? Fire is useful — what for? How did people make fires long ago? Who has a fire at home? What sort? Look for warning labels on clothes and furniture. What do they indicate?

Science Activities

Set up simple controlled experiment. Observe what happens to different fabrics when burned.

Show how fire needs oxygen to burn.

Art and Craft

Marbling pictures — red/yellow background — cut out silhouettes of buildings, people, fire engines and glue to background.

Colour mixing — begin with painted yellow flame shape at bottom of paper. Follow outline of shape, adding a little more red to paint each time until all the paper is filled.

Red and yellow wavy patterns — use bright red/yellow or fluorescent paint. Paint a wavy line down one side of paper. Continue in sequence pattern.

Collage — use fabrics, foils, Cellophanes, lametta and glitter on black or white paper. Spatter fluorescent red/yellow over top of collage.

Maths

Make models of fire engines. What shapes have you used? Can the fire engine move? How can you fit a flashing light?

How many fire extinguishers are there in your school?

Other Language Ideas

Vocabulary — fiery, crackling, red-hot, fierce, raging, burning, furnace.

Use descriptive words to build up a poem.

Books and Stories

Fighting a Fire by Brenda Williams in 'Stepping Stones', Kingfisher.

The Little Match Girl illustrated by Rachel Isadora, Picture Knight.

Poems and Rhymes

'The Dreadful Story about Harriet and the Matches', from *Struwelpeter,* by Dr. Heinrich Hoffman, Routledge and Kegan Paul.

'The Sound of Fire' by Mary O'Neill in *Singing in the Sun,* Young Puffin.

Songs and Music

'Camp Fires Burning' in *Brown Bread and Butter,* Ward Lock Educational.

Picture to look at

'A Cottage by Firelight, York', Mary Ellen Best, c. 1836.

Display Board

Background — yellow. Border marbled and cut to give flame effect. Letters of 'fire' — marbled in red and yellow. Large fire collage in centre — made from Cellophanes, foils, tissue and left-over marbling pictures (flames).

Display Table

Red and yellow fabric plus orange net. Models/toy fire engines, fire experiment with candle and jar; doll, dressed as 'cave dweller', rubbing sticks together. Large fire-fighter — child's playsuit stuffed with newspaper, tissue paper head, real hose and plastic helmet.

Bubbles

Discussion and Observation/Science Ideas
What is a bubble? Blow a bubble into the air. What do you see? What colours can you see? What happens to it? Look for bubbles elsewhere — bubble packing, fizzy drinks, chocolate bars, milkshakes, washing-up liquid, bubble bath, shampoo, hair mousse, glass paper weights. Can you see the air bubbles trapped inside?

Science/Cooking Ideas
Talk about the need for air bubbles in certain cooked foods, e.g. to help cakes rise. How do we get air bubbles into food? Look at different kinds of whisks — balloon, rotary, electric.
Make meringues — observe and discuss the effect of whisking raw egg whites.

Maths
Working in twos, blow bubbles outside. Whose floats the highest/lasts the longest? Who can blow the biggest bubble?
Circles and spheres. Look for other spherical objects.

Art and Craft
Bubble printing.
Bubble effect printing — use toilet roll tubes, yoghurt pots or variety of small cylindrical shapes.
Circle collage — use shiny paper, metallic foils, translucent gift wraps (could overprint collage with circles).

Other Language Ideas
Vocabulary — blow, pop, burst, float, froth, light, airy, transparent, translucent, opaque, foamy.
Describe having a bubble bath.

Books and Stories
'The witches' chant, from *Macbeth,* Act 1, Scene i.
Fun with Science by Brenda Walpole, Kingfisher.
Mother's Magic by Susan Hill, Picture Lion.
A Book about Bubbles by Helen Arnold, from Level 1 of 'Reading for Learning', Macmillan Education.

Poems and Rhymes
'Bubbles', by L. Nicholson, *The Book of a Thousand Poems,* Bell & Hyman.
'Billy's bath' by Clive Riche, *A Very First Poetry Book,* OUP.

Songs and Music
'I'm forever blowing bubbles', *Ta-ra-ra Boom-de-ay,* A & C Black.
'Blowing Bubbles', *Sixty Songs for Little Children,* OUP.
'Soap Bubbles' from *Jeux d'enfants,* Georges Bizet.

Picture to look at
'Bubbles', Millais.

Display Board
Pale blue background, darker blue border. Letters of 'bubbles' cut out of spare bubble prints.

Display Table
Pale pink and violet shiny fabric; tank of bubbles, pots of bubbles, meringues, whisks, aerated chocolate bars, spherical objects, books and stories.

Holes and Gaps

a set of dangerous holes

Can you think of any more?

Discussion and Observation/Science Ideas

Holes are all around us — can you find any? Holes on ourselves — faces, scalp and skin. Clothes holes — pockets, armholes, neck holes, button holes, patterns in fabric. Useful holes/useless holes. Dangerous holes — plug sockets, broken windows, pot holes etc.

People who work in holes or tunnels underground — miners, underground train drivers, sewage workers. What raw materials come from underground? Making holes — drills, excavators, hole punch, gimlet. Mending holes — what can be used to mend different kinds of holes? Animal holes.

Other Science Ideas

Find suitable materials to mend a variety of holes — puncture, hole in jumper, trousers or socks, paddling pool, knee.

Kitchen holes — find examples of useful holes in the kitchen — plughole, sieve, colander, bin etc.

Art and Craft

Hole prints — print with toilet rolls or other cylindrical shapes in a variety of colours.

Keyhole pictures — what can you see through the keyhole?

Stencils — make own or use doilies.

Fold gummed paper circles into eighths — cut out and make into collage pattern on bright paper.

Paper weaving.

Line drawings of hole patterns on shoes.

Visit art gallery to see sculptures. Can you see the holes?

Make own hole sculpture with clay, dough or Plasticine.

Cooking Activities

Make 'ring' cake. Fill hole with fruit or ice cream.

Have a 'Hole Food' tea! — doughnuts, polo mints, iced ring biscuits, potato rings, spaghetti rings. Stress importance of thorough cleaning of teeth in order to prevent 'holes' in teeth caused by 'hole food'.

Maths

Do holes have to be round? Find holes in different shapes and sizes.

Draw different shaped holes.

Bring in a honeycomb. What shapes do you see? Do they tessellate?

Draw own tessellation — which shapes tessellate?

Holes and Gaps

Other Language Ideas

Vocabulary — nook, crevice, cranny, fissure, orifice, gap, opening, burrow, den, earth, lair, nest.

Expressions — 'pick holes in', 'hole in a corner', 'what a hole', 'hole in one'.

Look for places with 'hole' or 'hol' in the name — Holborn, Mousehole, Wookey Hole, Hutton-le-hole, Foxholes.

Read *The Very Hungry Caterpillar*. Make own concertina book with similar theme.

Books and Stories

Holes and Peeks by Ann Jones, Julia Macrae Books.

'The Hole in the Sky', Polish Tale in *Listen to this,* compiled by Laura Cecil, Bodley Head.

'A Hole in Your Stocking' by Diana Ross in *In a Golden Land,* ed. by James Reeves, Young Puffin.

The Very Hungry Caterpillar by Eric Carle, Picture Puffin.

Mrs. Plug the Plumber, Allan Ahlberg and Joe Wright, Puffin Books.

Poems and Rhymes

'There's a Hole in the Middle of the Sea', Anon, in *Rhyme Time,* Barbara Ireson, Beaver Books.

'My Garden' by B. Ireson in *Rhyme Time,* Barbara Ireson, Beaver Books.

'Holes of Green' by Aileen Fisher in *A First Poetry Book,* OUP.

Songs and Music

'There's a Hole in my Bucket, *Appuskidu,* A & C Black.

'The Mole' in *The Clarendon Book of Singing Games,* Book I, OUP.

'Winter Food Stores' in *Birds and Beasts,* A & C Black.

'Mr. Minnitt' by Rose Fyleman in *Third Sixty Songs for Little Children,* OUP.

Sculptures to look at

Look at sculptures by Barbara Hepworth (Tate Gallery).

Display Board

Green background, large white keyhole shape in centre. Border of 'hole' prints (on white paper). Letters of 'holes' — bright orange on green (punch out holes to make pattern on letters). Figure of child dressed in real clothes as shown.

Display Table

Orange fabric. Books, sieves, colanders, macaroni, potato rings, slatted spoons, anything with holes.

Rubbish?

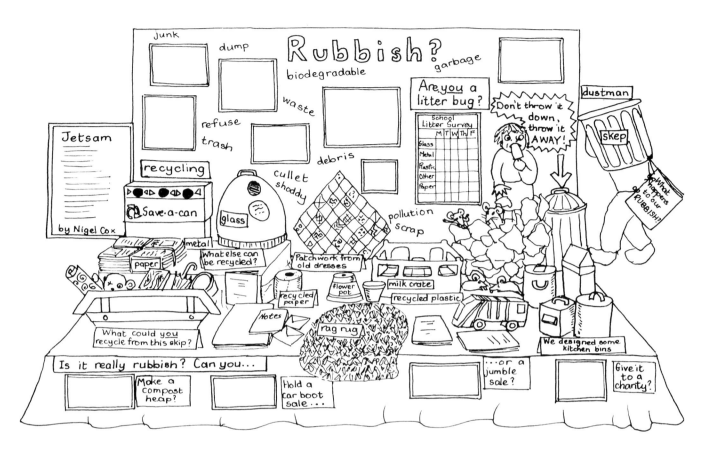

Discussion and Observation/Science Ideas

Sing 'The Tidy Song' and 'Litter Song'. What is litter? Is litter the same as rubbish? Where is rubbish found and where does it come from?

Pollution — how does rubbish pollute the environment? What can we do to prevent this happening? Carry out a litter survey in school grounds/street — wear old, thick gloves to collect litter. Put rubbish into a box or carrier bag. Sort litter into groups — plastic, paper, metal, glass. How much litter is from food products?

Visit department store or supermarket and look at examples of unnecessary packaging, particularly in toys. What do you throw away at home? Observe and record what rubbish is thrown away at home during one week. Can any be recycled? Why recycle anything? Find out about:

a) Local bottle banks and glass recycling.
b) Newspaper collections for paper recycling.
c) Local save-a-can recycling schemes.
d) Any charities which collect foil, paper, wool scraps, used clothes. How are they recycled?
e) Recycled plastic.

How can we recycle our own rubbish? Jumble or Car Boot sales; make collages, junk models or toys; make compost heaps from kitchen or garden waste.

Find examples in shops of products made from recycled materials.

Observe refuse collectors at work. What do they wear? Describe sounds and smells. What happens to the collected rubbish?

Carry out a 'bin survey' in the locality — how many litter bins are there? Where are they located? Are there sufficient and are they well designed?

Discuss the dangers of playing in rubbish dumps.

Art and Craft

Use waste plastics to make collages; also scrap metal, wood or paper.

Design poster and logo on anti-litter, or to encourage recycling.

Simple weaving with scrap plastics and paper.

Paintings of refuse collectors and dustcarts.

Use empty plastic bottles to make vases, boats, skittles, dolls. Glue on strips of thin lining paper. Paint, decorate, varnish.

Look at kitchen bins in a department store. Which are best designed and why? Draw own designs and make models in paper, card or plastic.

Design a machine that clears up and disposes of litter. What does it look like? How does it work? Use crayons, felt-tips or oil pastels.

Rubbish?

What would you do with your rubbish...

...if no-one ever came to collect it?

Maths

Sort clean rubbish into sets.

Weigh amounts of rubbish found in survey.

Capacity — how much rubbish will fit into different sized bins?

Arrange kitchen bins in order of size. Estimate which is heaviest. Weigh in kilogrammes. Can you lift it when it is empty? Weigh it when full of newspapers/bricks.

Put results of litter survey on weekly graph. Do amounts of litter found decrease in response to a school anti-litter campaign?

Other Language Ideas

Write class letter or individual letters to manufacturer pointing out excessive packaging and asking for modifications.

Write to shops asking them to stock more recycled goods and to state on the pack if they contain recycled materials.

Vocabulary — 'task and finish', filler, short crew, weighbridge, skep, hopper, compactor, shoddy, cullet, recycle, biodegradable; different words for rubbish.

How was rubbish dealt with long ago? What were living conditions like as a result?

Make up anti-litter slogans.

Other Ideas

Organise collection of items for recycling.

Book and Stories

War on Waste by Joy Palmer, Dryad Press Ltd.

The Dustman by Anne Stewart, 'Cherrystones' Series, Hamish Hamilton.

The Tale of Georgie Grubb by Jeanne Willis, Scholastic.

Joachim the Dustman by Kurt Baumann and David McKee, A & C Black.

Scrap Materials by Mike Roussell, Wayland.

Poems and Rhymes

'The Dustbin Men' by Gregory Harris in *A First Poetry Book*, OUP.

'Jetsam' by Nigel Cox in *Another First Poetry Book*, OUP.

Songs and Music

'Litter Song' by Josie Bradley in *Mrs. Macaroni*, Macmillan Educational.

'Tidy Song' by Sandra Kerr in *Tinderbox*, A & C Black.

'The Dustbin Men' in *Silly Aunt Sally*, Ward Lock.

Display Board

Background — any bright colour. Letters of 'rubbish?' cut from newspaper backed with black. Children's pictures backed in black and/or contrasting colour. Staple collage figure to board and variety of litter around her. **Dustbin** — card covered in foil, bent outwards to give 3D effect.

Figure of dustman and skep. Attach book of children's writing.

Display Table

Cover to match board. Cardboard models of bottle bank, skip and 'save-a-can'.

Other items as shown.

Kitchen Machines

Discussion and Observation/Science Ideas

What is a machine? How can they make life easier? What machines are in your home? How do they work? Different forms of power — gas, electricity, hand, water, wind, animal or steam. Which are used at home? How do they reach our homes?

Look at the inside of an old machine. Ask local electrician, repair person or parent to explain how it works.

Visit a museum to see domestic appliances, old and new. How do they differ? How were domestic tasks carried out before they were performed by machines?

Focus on one particular appliance/machine which each home has. Ask children and parents to comment on its performance, design, reliability. Record results.

Discuss commonsense rules concerning gas, electricity, fire, sharp edges.

Art and Craft

Make collages from small parts and scrap from machines, glued on to card or pressed into meat tray filled with plaster of Paris.

Design own 'invention' — what does it do, and how does it work? Use pencils or felt-tip pens. Look at Heath Robinson cartoons for inspiration.

Use machine parts/scrap to build own 'machine' or invention, or simply a machine sculpture. Use masking tape, adhesive tape, string or wire to join pieces together.

Print with machine parts — cogs, springs etc.

Line drawings of machines — outside or inside. Use pencils, felt-tips pens, Conté crayons.

Maths

How much time do machines save?

How long do machines last before breaking down?

What is the biggest/smallest machine in your home?

Find out costs/running costs of different appliances.

Are your electricity/gas bills higher in winter? Why? How could you make your bills smaller?

Other Language Ideas

Talk about/write about the machine you would like to invent. What would it do? How would it work? Is it safe to use?

Vocabulary — names of machines, electrical terms.

Survey — which domestic machines are felt to be necessities/useful/pure luxury? Record results.

Dance/Drama

Group work — make up a 'machine' dance to suitable music — short, sharp, jerky movements; 'robotic' dancing.

Mime people using machines and appliances to perform household tasks.

Kitchen Machines

Musical Activities

Make machine sounds using home-made instruments, everyday metal and plastic objects, body percussion.

Books and Stories

Home Inventions, by Molly Harrison, Usborne.

Doing the Washing, by Sarah Garland, Picture Puffin.

Emma and the Vacuum Cleaner, by Gunilla Wolde, Hodder and Stoughton.

Norma and the Washing Machine, by Michael Rosen, André Deutsch.

Poems and Rhymes

'My Toaster', by Barbara Ireson in *Funny Rhymes,* Arrow Books Ltd.

'A Fridge', by Martyn Wiley and Ian MacMillan in *Another Firsty Poetry Book,* OUP.

'Our Washing Machine', by Patricia Hubbell in *The Walker Book of Poetry for Children,* Walker Books.

Songs and Music

'Dashing away with the Smoothing Iron', in *Strawberry Fair,* A & C Black.

'Machines' by David Moses, in *Kokoleoko,* Macmillan Educational.

'The Washerwomen' in *The Clarendon Book of Singing Games, Book 1,* OUP.

Pictures to look at

'Kitchen at Langton', Mary Ellen Best, 1830's.

'Kitchen of the Hotel St. Lucan in Hoogstraat, Rotterdam', Mary Ellen Best, 1834.

Display Board

Background — bright yellow. Children's pictures of machines backed in black or contrasting colour. Letters of 'Kitchen machines' — cut from fluorescent orange or red, backed in black. Cut-out male figure dressed in old clothes, stuffed with newspaper and stapled to board.

Display Table

Yellow fabric cover. Make appliances from strong boxes, painted white and coated with PVA. Use stick-on Velcro for door fastenings.

Oven and hob — cut door for oven. Tape in shelf. Paint radiant rings on to hob. Cut circles from thick card for knobs; paint, and attach with split pins. **Washing machine** — cut porthole door. Use clear acetate for glass. **Fridge** — tape in shelf. Glue pictures of food to inside of door. Position plastic or dough 'food' inside fridge. Make **toaster** from junk materials. Paint foam pieces to represent burnt toast. Paint smoke on board. Toy ironing board and iron. Clothes, models of food, toy crockery and cutlery, book of own recipes, as shown.

For details of further Belair publications,
please write to: Libby Masters,
BELAIR PUBLICATIONS LIMITED,
Albert House, Apex Business Centre,
Boscombe Road, Dunstable, LU5 4RL.

For sales and distribution in North America and South America
INCENTIVE PUBLICATIONS,
3835 Cleghorn Avenue, Nashville, Tn 37215.
USA.

For sales and distribution in Australia
EDUCATIONAL SUPPLIES PTY LTD
8 Cross Street, Brookvale, NSW 2100.
Australia

For sales and distribution (in other territories)
FOLENS PUBLISHERS
Albert House, Apex Business Centre,
Boscombe Road, Dunstable, LU5 4RL.
United Kingdom.
E-mail: folens@folens.com